NAPOLEON

Historical Enigma

PROBLEMS IN CIVILIZATION

NAPOLEON

Historical Enigma

Edited with
an Introduction by

David H. Pinkney

University of Washington

FORUM PRESS

Library of Congress Catalog Card Number: 77-76609

ISBN: 0-88273-403-2

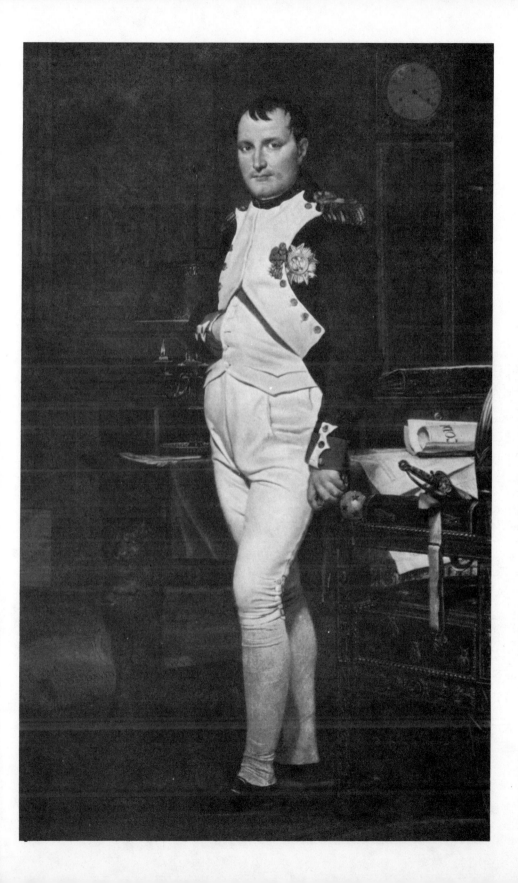

CONTENTS

IV. ENLIGHTENED DESPOT OR MODERN DICTATOR?

INTRODUCTION

Each day scores of buses, from every country of Western Europe, draw up to the Place Vauban in Paris and disgorge a flood of tourists who have come to see the Tomb of Napoleon. Once inside the Chapel of the Invalides they find no more than the great bulk of the Emperor's red marble sarcophagus, the tombs of some of his family and his lieutenants, and a few relics — not a very exciting display. Yet so great is the fascination evoked by the memory of this extraordinary man that a century and a half after his death his tomb is one of the chief tourist attractions in an attraction-filled city. Scarcely a year passes, moreover, without a Napoleonic exposition at one of the city's museums, and each year the presses of Europe and America add a score or more titles to the amazing Napoleonic bibliography, which at the turn of the century already exceeded 100,000 items.

The fascination of Napoleon for historians at least matches that which he holds for the layman. The Emperor was not yet in his grave when historians began writing about him, and they have never relaxed their interest nor their pens. Part of the attraction springs from the very incredibility of his career — an unknown general in 1795, a year later at the age of twenty-seven, the brilliantly successful commander of the army of Italy, and two years after that the leader of an army fighting in the shadow of the pyramids of Egypt; soon the pacifier of a war-torn continent and skillful reformer at home, the conqueror of Europe while still in his thirties; then followed his rapid decline and fall and ultimate exile on a rock in the South Atlantic. He left his impress on every country of Europe, and no history of the nineteenth century can ignore the consequences of his career. Napoleon would be a major focus of historians' concern for these reasons alone, and even if they sought only to reconstruct his life. But beyond the simple facts, the historiography of Napoleon is alive with controversy. Beginning with the very earliest historians of Napoleon, there has been debate over many aspects of his career — his motives, his objectives at home and abroad, his relationship to the Revolution, his mistakes, his military abilities, his lasting contributions to France and to Europe. Historians' changing judgments of the man were usually influenced by the political climate and debates of their own times, and thus history and political controversy have frequently been confounded in their studies.

The first historians — Chateaubriand, Madame de Staël, Mignet — were unfavorably disposed toward the Emperor, but as the memories of his wars and his infringements on personal freedoms faded and the glories of the Empire were magnified by time and by contrast with the drabness of its successors, historians became more kindly toward him. They were influenced, too, by the skillful reconstruction of his career that Napoleon and his aides fashioned on Saint-Helena. In this reconstruction, the so-called Napoleonic Legend, Napoleon appeared as the defender of the Revolution and of the sovereignty of the people, the champion of equality, the savior of religion, the friend of nationalities, and the lover of peace who was the victim of the implacable fears and hatred of the conservative rulers of Europe and of the envy of Britain. Thiers, writing in the 1840's, '50's, and '60's under the influence of the Legend, produced the first great popular history of the Consulate and the Empire. Although not uncritical, it was generally favorable in its judgments of Napoleon and tried to excuse his faults. In the 1860's a reaction developed against the Emperor inspired, at least in part, by the experience of a Second Empire and another Napoleon and the renewed realization that strong government and liberty do not go together. After 1870 admiration for Napoleon revived in some circles, reflecting dismay at the miserable military showing of France in the Franco-Prussian War, (which contrasted so sharply with the military glories of Napoleon), hostility to England in the new colonial struggle, and conservative resentment at the rebirth of republican and parliamentary government. In the twentieth century conservative, nationalist, and literary historians of the *Académie francaise*, such as Bainville and Madelin, continued to write admiringly of him, while the republican historians associated with the University, Aulard and Lefebvre among them, were generally unsympathetic, reflecting the anti-militarism, in part a result of the Dreyfus Affaire, and the internationalism of republican intellectuals.

In the latter-twentieth century, historians associated with the journal *Annales: Economies-Societes-Civilisations*, who find the essence of history in long-term changes in climate, population, economies, and society, have minimized Napoleon's importance, holding that he had little influence on the deeply-based tendencies of French and European history. Out of the myriad volumes devoted to Napoleon has come no consensus, only continuing debate. Considering the vast literature the Dutch historian Pieter Geyl concluded, "History can reach no unchallengeable conclusions on so many-sided a character. . . ."

This volume concentrates on four much debated questions in the historiography of Napoleon. First, is he properly regarded as the defender and consolidator of the Revolution or did he destroy it? Second, was he an aggressor whose ambition for territory knew virtually no bounds or was he the guardian of his country's national frontiers, forced by the jealousy and the interference of rival powers into wars beyond the limits he would choose for France? Third, was Napoleon a military genius, one of the great commanders of all time, or only an unusually successful revolutionary general who managed to eliminate his rivals? Finally, was he a man of the past, the last of the Enlightened Despots, or the harbinger of a new type of political leader, the first of the modern dictators?

Napoleon himself was the first to contend that he was the defender of the Revolution. Emmanuel de Las Cases, one of his companions on Saint-Helena, quoted in his *Memorial de Saint-Hélène* from a history that Napoleon had begun to write on Elba; in it the Emperor pictured himself as the man who saved the Revolution from its enemies and consolidated and made permanent the benefits that it had brought to the French people, and at the same time reestablished national unity among all classes and parties. Madame de Staël, whom Napoleon had forced into exile, saw the Emperor quite differently. In her judgment he took advantage of France's exhaustion from war and bloodshed at home and abroad and of the French people's yearning for order and tranquility to impose a dictatorship upon the country. Of the entire Revolutionary heritage he retained only himself, and behind a facade of pseudo-representative bodies he deprived France of both liberty and equality and diverted her energies to foreign war as a further support of his despotism. Adolphe Thiers took a more favorable view. He saw the Consulate and the Empire as a second stage of the French Revolution in which Napoleon, after first condemning the excesses of its earlier stage — regicide, civil war, religious schism — and attempting to heal the wounds it had inflicted, encountered opposition and resorted to excesses himself. Nevertheless, he gave to France the definitive accomplishment of two great reforms initiated in the first stage of the Revolution — the law codes and an efficient administration. Edgar Quinet, writing during the Second Empire and expressing his disdain for both Napoleons, pictured the Consulate and the First Empire as a revival of the Carolingian and Byzantine Empires, in which the state and a subordinate church combined to deprive men of their liberties. Surviving in France after Napoleon's consolidation of his power were only the ruins of the Revolution's great effort of emancipation. Alphonse Aulard, a professional historian who aspired to scientific objectivity but whose writing was nonetheless influenced by his republicanism, saw Napoleon establishing a despotism that undid almost all the political results of the Revolution, but in his confirmation of the ownership of the National Lands and in his law codes he retained the basic social changes effected by the Revolution, and he can, therefore, be called "the man of the Revolution."

Consideration of the debate over Napoleon's foreign policy can well begin with Thiers, who in the 1860's presented an interpretation that continued to influence historians' judgments long after his time. During his years as First Consul, in Thiers' view, Napoleon pursued a policy aimed at achieving security for France and peace for Europe, but in 1803 and 1804 he allowed his resentment against England and his desire to humiliate her to deflect him from this policy. He provoked a general European war, won a spectacular victory over Austria and Russia at Austerlitz and again had an opportunity to make a continental peace and to isolate England. But, carried away by boundless ambition, he spurned the opportunity and turned instead to trying to establish a new Roman Empire.

In the final decade of the nineteenth century and the first of the twentieth a number of historians published books in which they attempted to explain Napoleon's foreign policy. The most famous of these was Albert Sorel's *L'Europe et la Révolution française*. In it he sought to show the continuity between the foreign policy of the Bourbons and the policies of the Revolutionary governments and of the Empire. Napoleon, he held, continued the policies of the monarchy, the Committee of Public Safety, and the Directory, aimed at expanding France to the frontiers of Gaul. He went beyond these limits only to assure that France's enemies would respect them. England, especially, insisted on France's withdrawal to the old frontiers of the monarchy and on the recall of the Bourbons, conditions unacceptable to France. It was England, too, who inspired the resistance of the continental powers and forced Napoleon into continual wars that he did not seek and did not want. Arthur Lévy was even more insistent on Napoleon's commitment to peace. He accepted Napoleon's own contention on Saint-Helena that he was sincerely and unremittingly devoted to the cause of peace, and he marshalled an array of documentary evidence to support it. For France Napoleon sought only the recognition of her natural frontiers and respect for her independence, and he worked unceasingly to arrange a general peace settlement, an effort in which he was foiled by the rival powers of Europe, especially by England, who would not tolerate a great and prosperous France under a revolutionary dynasty. Edouard Driault disputed the efforts to explain Napoleon's policy as a continuation of those of the Revolutionary governments. According to Driault, Napoleon was much more than a successor of Danton and Carnot; he pursued a very personal policy. He was no respecter of natural frontiers, and early in his career as well as later his ambitions extended far beyond them. He was the heir of the Roman Empire, ambitious to rule over the Mediterranean Sea, in which effort he was foiled by

the British. Forced to turn his energies to central Europe, he made himself the successor of Charlemagne without ever abandoning however, his desire to rule the Mediterranean.

All of these writers sought some principle that would permit a single coherent explanation of Napoleon's many activities in foreign affairs. Pierre Muret in commenting on them questioned the validity of all explanations that attribute a definite plan of expansion or conquest to Napoleon. His foreign policy is best understood, Muret concluded, as a succession of personal reactions to circumstances.

Although there is some articulate dissent, historians generally have recognized Napoleon as a military genius. Thiers, characteristically an admirer, came out firmly on that side. To him Napoleon was a military genius rivaled in all recorded history only by Hannibal. His genius was evident in his conduct of battles, in his organization of his forces, and in his handling of men. It was fully proven in his first campaigns in the Italian Expedition of 1796, and throughout his career he maintained the genius he first demonstrated there. His mistakes were political; his military failures are explicable not as the consequence of errors in military judgment but as the result of his overreaching himself as a political figure. Thiers also considers and denies the charge that Napoleon was only a general of the offensive and did not know how to handle armies in retreat and adversity. Yorck von Wartenburg, the German military historian, found in Napoleon the rare combination of, on the one hand, the ability to lead troops in the field and to inspire boundless confidence and personal devotion with, on the other, the mastery of theoretical strategy worked out in the seclusion of his headquarters. Many generals had one ability or the other, but Napoleon's combination of them, together with his ability to adapt his strategic conceptions to circumstances, made him "the greatest military genius." His weakness was his own self-deception: Originally basing his actions on clear understanding of facts, he came in his later years to ignore facts in his growing conviction that to him nothing was impossible. The historian Albert Guérard, no military specialist himself, refused to be overawed by Napoleon's great reputation among the military experts. He emphasized that Napoleon emerged prominently on the French scene only after the great work of reorganizing the French army had been accomplished by Carnot and his associates, and that then he appeared merely as one good general among half a dozen. Three of his rivals were removed by death, and the others were forced into exile or obscurity by the ambitious Napoleon. Without real rivals he appeared a giant, but he was no creative military genius. He used methods inherited from the revolutionary armies, and when, with characteristic lack of imagination, he tried to apply them in a environment — Russia — for which they were not suited, the result was disaster, a disaster for which Napoleon alone was responsible. Not until 1814, moreover, did he have to face a united enemy, and then he was defeated. Alfred Vagts, a military historian, saw Napoleon as perhaps a military genius but one who, as his career advanced, became increasingly cut off from reality and increasingly reckless in his use of large numbers of men, a practice that led to his downfall.

Some historians see Napoleon's rule as the last blooming of eighteenth-century despotism and Napoleon as a man of that century. Others view him as the first of a new type of popular dictator. Georges Lefebvre, in a complex analysis of Napoleon's character and motives, notes that he prided himself on basing his actions on rational analysis of facts, placing himself in the tradition of eighteenth-century rationalism. The threat of counter-revolution forced him, as it had forced all his predecessors since 1793, to believe that authoritarian government was at least temporarily essential, but he also believed in the revolutionary reforms that had put an end to the remnants of feudalism and to civil inequality in France. He sought to reconcile authority and reform in a revival of enlightened despotism, and he is best understood as "the last and the most illustrious" of the Enlightened Despots. Geoffrey Bruun holds that to appreciate Napoleon's role in its proper historical perspective one must keep in mind that politically the eighteenth century was the age of enlightened despots who shared a common commitment to codify laws aimed at abolishing feudal institutions

such as guilds, corporations, and provincial estates, and at establishing efficient and vigorous central administrations. These included the essential aims and achievements of Napoleon in his domestic rule, and he is in this respect much more a philosopher prince, a man of the eighteenth-century Enlightenment, than he is a man of the Revolution or a new kind of modern dictator. Frederick Artz looks ahead half a century and more from 1799 to find regimes similar to Napoleon's. He first points out similarities between the rule of Napoleon I and that of his nephew, Napoleon III, who reestablished the Empire in 1852. Going beyond the Second Empire he compares both the Bonapartist regimes with the fascist dictatorships of the twentieth century. Here, too, he finds similarities but also many important, although less evident, differences. In Alfred Cobban's judgment, France in 1799, after ten years of revolutionary upheaval, needed a strong leader, and Napoleon filled the need. He imposed himself on France as the man of the army, but the concept of popular sovereignty was still so firmly entrenched in France that he felt the need for popular sanction of his rule, and this he sought through plebiscites. The plebiscites endorsed his seizure of supreme power and established the idea that one man can assume all the powers of a despot in the name of the will of the people. "The idea of sovereignty, freed from all restraints, and transferred to the people," Cobban declared, "had at last given birth to the first modern dictatorship."

No unchallengeable answers to the questions posed in this volume are likely to arise from the reading of the selections offered or indeed from the reading of any balanced sampling of the literature on Napoleon. But they will suggest something of the rich variety of Napoleon's career that permits such divergent views, and they will reveal some of the vitality of the long and continuing debate over Napoleon and perhaps help to explain the unfailing attraction of historians and amateurs alike to him. Moreover, the search for answers to these questions should stimulate thought not only about Napoleon and his career but also about the nature of history and the possibilities of drawing conclusions from historical evidence.

Conflict of Opinion

"I have stopped up the abyss of anarchy, and produced order out of chaos. I have cleansed the Revolution, ennobled the nations, strengthened the throne."

—— Napoleon

"But Bonaparte conceived the idea of using the counter-revolution to his advantage by retaining in the state, so to speak, nothing new except himself. He reestablished the throne, the clergy, and the nobility; a monarchy, as Pitt said, without legitimacy and without limits; a clergy that was only the preacher of despotism; a nobility composed of old and new families but which performed no civic function in the state and served only as an ornament of the absolute power."

—— Mme. de Staël

"The imperial despotism stopped the Revolution, marked a retreat toward the principles of the *ancien régime,* provisionally abolished liberty, partially abolished equality. However, these are the political results of the Revolution rather than the social results that were thus suppressed. Possession of national lands, civil laws compiled in a code . . . imposed on almost all Europe — that is how the social results of the Revolution survived, and it is that which explains that after his fall, when these results were challenged by the royalist émigrés, this Napoleon Bonaparte, who had undone the political work of the Revolution in so far as he could, appeared to be and could call himself the man of the Revolution."

—— Alphonse Aulard

"Everything was faulty in the arrangements in Vienna in 1806, but Napoleon did not confine himself to these mistakes, already so grave. When he returned to Paris, an intoxication of ambition, unknown in modern times, usurped his mind. Henceforth, he thought of an immense empire, supported by vassal kingdoms, which would dominate Europe and would be designated by a name consecrated by the Romans and by Charlemagne, Empire of the West."

—— Adolphe Thiers

"The provisional executive council, in 1792, had designated the Rhine as the frontier of the Republic; the Committee of Public Safety of the Year III had negotiated the cession of that frontier to France. In order to obtain it, to indemnify the German princes dispossessed on the left bank, it had proposed the secularization of the ecclesiastical principalities of the right bank. . . . It had foreseen the necessity of combining the continent against England in order to force it to recognize France's possession of the frontiers of Gaul. . . . Bonaparte is nourished on this. . . . France expects of him the accomplishment of the design that is for her the condition and the guarantee of peace, the termination of the Revolution, the triumph and splendor of the Republic. . . . It is the master thought, the permanent object of his policy. . . ."

—— Albert Sorel

"The thorough study of documents, particularly those conserved in foreign chancelleries, proves that the responsibility for fifteen years of war under the Consulate and Empire cannot be placed upon Napoleon. On the contrary, during all his reign he had as his sole objective the conclusion of an equitable, solid peace, assuring France the rank that was her due.

"The immutable English rivalry, the fright of the ancient thrones confronted with an upstart dynasty, the hope of raising a barrier against the expansion of the idea of liberty, the secret covetousness of all, such are the elements out of which were formed the successive coalitions and against which beat unceasingly the pacific efforts of Napoleon."

—— Arthur Lévy

"There was now another Charlemagne, with more splendor, more genius: 'I did not succeed Louis XIV,' he said, 'but Charlemagne.'"

—— Edouard Driault

"It leads us, indeed, in terminating our study to pose a question, which all the recent historians of Napoleon in France supposed resolved and which, in our view, is by no means resolved. Is it certain that the Napoleonic policy had a defined objective? Did there exist a grand Napoleonic plan susceptible of being precisely stated?"

—— Pierre Muret

"He lacked nothing of mind or character necessary to the true captain, and one can sustain the proposition that if Hannibal had not existed he would probably be without equal."

—— Adolphe Thiers

"Under the Convention miracles were accomplished, but Napoleon was still obscure. Under the Directoire and the Consulate, he had forged to the front rank, but remained only *primus inter pares,* with such peers as Hoche, Kléber, Desaix, Masséna, Moreau. His chief advantage over most of them was his craftier and more ruthless ambition; his decisive advantage over the three noblest is that they died and he lived."

—— Albert Guérard

"As his egomania grew in size, he lost all sense of the proportions among things and of the limitations on human power, however great it may be at a given moment. . . . In Napoleon's case it meant more than a loosening of his mental and physical grip on the material and human resources at his command. It meant a blind and stubborn incapacity to understand the imponderables in front of him."

—— Alfred Vagts

"Napoleon lent his name to an epoch because he symbolized reason enthroned, because he was the philosopher-prince who gave to the dominant aspiration of the age its most typical, most resolute, and most triumphant expression."

—— Geoffrey Bruun

Conflict of Opinion

"The analogies between the Bonapartist regimes and the Fascist dictatorships are obvious. All arose out of political and social crises. . . . All promise all things to all men, all make use of a sense of tarnished national glory, all use wars and war scares to keep themselves in power. All perfect the secret police and the censorship; . . . all are backed by the army; all are sanctioned by the ritual of the plebescite. All perish in war."

—— FREDERICK B. ARTZ

I. DEFENDER OR DESTROYER OF THE REVOLUTION?

Man of the Legend

EMMANUEL DE LAS CASES

Emmanuel, Comte de Las Cases (1766–1842), an officer of the royal navy, fled from France during the Revolution but returned in 1802 and rallied to Napoleon. He served in the Council of State, became the Emperor's chamberlain, and in 1815 accompanied his master into exile on Saint-Helena, where he remained until expelled by the British governor in December 1816. During his months in exile he collected and recorded the words of Napoleon, and on his return to France he incorporated them, along with an account of life on Saint-Helena, into a book, *Le Mémorial de Sainte-Hélène*, published in 1821 and soon translated into the principal European languages. It became the first great source of the Napoleonic Legend (and incidentally made a fortune for its compiler). The excerpt below is part of a history of France that Napoleon himself began while on Elba and never completed.

THE FIVE members of the Directory were divided among themselves; the enemies of the Republic insinuated themselves into the councils and brought into the government men who were enemies of the people. This form of government kept the state in ferment, and the great benefits that the French had gained in the Revolution were continually compromised. A unanimous voice issuing from the depths of the countryside, from the heart of the towns, from the bosom of the camps asked that while preserving all the principles of the Republic there be established within the government a hereditary system that sheltered the principles and the interests of the Revolution from the factions and the influence of foreigners. The First Consul of the Republic, by the Constitution of the Year VIII, held office for ten years; the nation extended his magistracy for the remainder of his life; it raised him to the throne, which it made hereditary in his family. The principles of sovereignty of the people, of liberty, of equality, of the destruction of the feudal regime, of the irrevocability of the sale of the national lands, of the freedom of religion were all consolidated. The government of France, under this fourth dynasty, was founded on the same principles as the Republic: it was a limited, constitutional monarchy. There was as much difference between the government of France under that fourth dynasty and the third as between the latter and the Republic. The fourth dynasty succeeded the Republic, or rather it was only a modification of it.

No prince mounted the throne with more legitimate rights than Napoleon. The throne was tendered to Hugh Capet by some bishops and some nobles; the imperial

From Emmanuel de Las Cases, *Le Mémorial de Sainte-Hélène* (Paris: Garnier Frères, n.d.), III, 430–434. [Editor's translation.]

1

throne was given to Napoleon by the will of all the citizens, verified three times in a solemn manner. Pope Pius VII, chief of the Roman, Catholic, and Apostolic religion, the religion of the majority of Frenchmen, crossed the Alps to anoint the Emperor with his own hands, surrounded by all the bishops of France, by all the cardinals of the Roman Church, and by the deputies of all the cantons of the Empire. The kings hastened to recognize him. All saw with pleasure this modification of the Republic, which put France in harmony with the rest of Europe, and consolidated the happiness and the situation of that great nation. The ambassadors of the Emperors of Austria and of Russia, those of Prussia, of Spain and Portugal, of Turkey, of America, and eventually all the powers came to compliment the Emperor. England alone sent no one, having violated the Treaty of Amiens and renewed the war with France; but even she approved these changes. Lord Whitworth, in the secret negotiations that took place through the intermediary of Count Malouet and that preceded the rupture of the peace of Amiens, proposed, on behalf of his government, to recognize Napoleon as King of France, if he would agree to the cession of Malta. The First Consul replied that if ever the well-being of France should require that he mount the throne, it would be only by the free and unaided will of the French people. When, later, Lord Lauderdale came to Paris, in 1806, to negotiate peace between the King of England and the Emperor, he exchanged credentials, as the protocol of the negotiations proves, and negotiated with the plenipotentiary of the Emperor. . . .

The Emperor bound up the wounds of the Revolution; all the émigrés returned and that list of proscribed persons was destroyed. The prince performed the most kindly glorious act, that of recalling to their country, and thus reestablishing, more than twenty thousand families. Their unsold property was returned to them; and wiping clean the slate of the past, he welcomed equally to all employments individuals of all the classes, whatever their conduct had been. The families who owed their positions to services rendered to the Bourbons, those who had been the most devoted to them, occupied places at Court, in the administration, and in the army. All titles were forgotten; there were no longer aristocrats or Jacobins, and the establishment of the Legion of Honor, which was the reward for military, civil, and judicial service, united side by side the soldier, the scholar, the artist, the prelate, and the magistrate; it was a symbol of reunion of all the estates, of all the parties.

Dictator

MADAME DE STAËL

Germaine Necker, Baronne de Staël-Holstein (1766–1817), known as Madame de Staël, was the daughter of the Swiss banker Jacques Necker, who was Louis XVI's chief minister from 1776 to 1781 and again in the first months of the Revolution. A prolific writer and the leader of an influential salon, she

From *Considérations sur les principaux événemens de la Révolution française*, Vol. XIII in *Oeuvres complètes de Mme La Baronne de Staël* (Paris: Treuttel et Wurtz, 1820–21), pp. 237–50, 258–59, 319–20. [Editor's translation.]

remained throughout her life loyal to the ideals of the early stages of the Revolution. She was at first an enthusiastic supporter of Napoleon, whom she thought of as a practitioner of those ideals. She was soon disillusioned, however, and being a literate and outspoken woman she was, in 1803, forced into exile, an exile that continued until 1814. She fled the country again when Napoleon returned from Elba and came back only in 1816. Out of this experience emerged her *Considérations sur la Révolution française*, completed after her return to France in 1814 and published in 1818 after her untimely death the preceding year.

IN THE committees of the Five Hundred, in the presence of the officers of his suite and of some friends of the Directors, General Bonaparte delivered a speech that was printed in the journals of the time. That speech offered a remarkable comparison that history should record. "What have they done?" he said, in speaking of the Directors, "with that brilliant France that I left them? I left them peace, and I found war; I left them victories, and I found defeats. Finally, what have they done with one hundred thousand Frenchmen all of whom I knew, my companions in arms, and who are now dead?" Then, terminating suddenly his harangue in a calmer tone, he added, "This state of things cannot last; it would lead us to despotism in three years." Bonaparte took upon himself to hasten the accomplishment of his prediction.

But would it not be a great lesson for the human race, if the Directors, very unwarlike men, should arise from the grave and demand an accounting from Napoleon for the frontiers of the Rhine and of the Alps, conquered by the Republic; an accounting for the foreigners' twice occupying Paris; an accounting for three million Frenchmen who perished from Cadiz to Moscow; an accounting especially for that sympathy that the nations felt for the cause of liberty in France, and which is now changed into a deeply rooted aversion? Certainly, the Directors would not be more deserving of praise for it; but one should conclude that in our time an enlightened nation can do nothing worse than to surrender itself into the hands of one man. The public now has more intelligence than any individual, and

institutions rally support much more wisely than circumstances. If the French nation, instead of choosing that fatal stranger, who exploited it for his own advantage, and foolishly exploited it even in that respect; if the French nation, I say, then so grand in spite of all its faults, had organized itself, respecting the lessons that ten years of experience had just given it, it would still be the light of the world.

The most potent magic that Bonaparte used to establish his power is, as we have already said, the terror inspired by the mere name of Jacobinism, although all men capable of reflection know perfectly well that that curse cannot revive in France. One readily assumes the air of fearing defeated parties in order to justify general measures of coercion. All those who want to favor the establishment of despotism recall vigorously the crimes committed by demagogues. It is a very easy tactic; thus Bonaparte paralyzed all resistance to his will by these words, "Do you want me to hand you over to the Jacobins?" And France then bowed before him, without any energetic men daring to reply, "We know how to fight Jacobins and you." In short he was not loved even then, but he was preferred; he almost always presented himself in opposition to another fear in order to have his power accepted as the lesser of two evils.

A commission, composed of fifty members of the Five Hundred and of the Ancients, was charged with discussing with General Bonaparte the constitution that was going to be proclaimed. Some of those members who had just the other day jumped out the window to escape bayonets seriously discussed the abstract questions of new laws, as if one could still assume that their authority would be respected. This *sang-froid* would have been fine if it had been combined with energy; but abstract questions were discussed only to establish a tyranny; as in the time of Cromwell when passages were sought in the Bible to justify absolute power.

Bonaparte let these men, accustomed to talking from the Tribune, dissipate in words the remains of their character; but when they approached, in theory, too close to the practical, he cut short all the difficulties by threatening to take no further part in their business; that is to say, to end it by force. He was agreeable enough in these long discussions because he himself loved to talk. His style of dissimulation in politics is not silence; he prefers to confuse men's minds by a whirlwind of talk that makes one believe in turn the most contradictory things. In fact, one often deceives better by speaking than by being silent. The least sign betrays those who remain silent; but, when one has the effrontery to lie actively, one can have more effect on convictions. Now Bonaparte lent himself to the quibbles of a committee that discussed the establishment of a social order like the composition of a book. It was not then a matter of former institutions to be treated with caution, of privileges to preserve, or even of usages to respect: the Revolution had so thoroughly deprived France of all memories of the past, that no antique foundation fettered the plan of the new constitution. . . .

Every evening we heard of the meetings of Bonaparte with his committee, and these reports could have amused us if they had not deeply saddened us concerning the fate of France. The courtier's servility of mind began to develop in men who had shown themselves the most ruggedly revolutionary. These ferocious Jacobins were rehearsing the roles of barons and counts for which they were destined, and everything announced that their personal interest would

be like Proteus, who assumed at will the most diverse shapes.

During that discussion I met a former member of the Convention whom I shall not name. . . . I expressed to him my concerns for liberty. "Oh, Madam," he replied, "we have reached the point of no longer thinking of saving the principles of the Revolution but only the men who made it." Certainly that wish was not the wish of France.

It was believed that Sieyès would present in complete form that famous constitution that had been talked about for ten years as the ark of the covenant that would unite all parties; but by a strange caprice he had written nothing on that subject. The superiority of Sieyès' mind could not prevail over the misanthropy of his character; the human race displeases him, and he does not know how to cope with it; it was said that he would like to deal with something other than men and that he renounces dealings because he cannot find on earth a species more to his taste. Bonaparte, who wasted his time neither in contemplation of abstract ideas nor in the discouragement of temperament, very quickly saw how Sieyès could be useful to him: it was in the skillful destruction of popular elections. Sieyès substituted for them lists of candidates from which the Senate was to choose the members of the Legislative Body and of the Tribunate; because there were in that constitution, I don't know why, three bodies and even four if one includes the Council of State, of which Bonaparte subsequently made such good use. When the choice of deputies is not made purely and directly by the people, the government is no longer representative; hereditary institutions can be combined with electoral institutions, but liberty consists of elections. The important thing for Bonaparte, therefore, was to paralyze popular elections because he knew that they were incompatible with despotism.

In that constitution, the Tribunate, composed of one hundred persons, was to speak, and the Legislative Body, composed of two hundred and fifty, was to be silent; but it is not clear why that permission was given to one and that constraint imposed upon the other. The Tribunate and the Legislative Body were not sufficiently numerous in proportion to the population of France; and all political importance was concentrated in the *Senat conservateur,* which combined all powers save one, that born of independence of wealth. The senators had no resources except the appointments they received from the executive power. The Senate was in effect only the mask of tyranny; it gave to the orders of a single man the appearance of having been discussed by many.

When Bonaparte was assured of having to deal only with paid men divided into three bodies and appointed by each other, he believed himself certain of achieving his goals. That glorious name of Tribune signified five-year pensions; that great name of Senator meant a benefice for life, and he understood very quickly that some wanted to acquire what the others desired to retain. Bonaparte made his will heard in various tones, sometimes in the sage voice of the Senate, sometimes by the enslaved cries of the Tribunes, sometimes by the silent vote of the Legislative Body; and that three-part choir was supposed to be the organ of the nation, although a single master was the director of them all.

The work of Sieyès was without doubt altered by Bonaparte. His long view, like that of a bird of prey, enabled him to discover and to suppress all that which could, in the proposed institutions, lead someday to some resistance; but Sieyès had destroyed liberty by providing a substitute for popular election.

Bonaparte by himself would perhaps not have been strong enough at the time to effect such a change in the generally accepted principles; philosophy had to serve the designs of the usurper. Not, certainly, that Sieyès wanted to establish tyranny in France, for justice requires us to admit that

he took no part in it; and, moreover, a man of such talent cannot like the authority of a single man, if that single man is not himself. But, by his metaphysic he confused the most simple question, that of election; and it was in the shadow of these clouds that Bonaparte found his way to despotism with impunity.

The first symptoms of tyranny cannot be too closely studied; because, when it has grown to a certain point, it cannot be stopped. A single man enchains the will of a multitude of individuals of whom most, taken separately, would wish to be free, but who, nonetheless, submit, because each of them fears the other and dares not communicate his thoughts to him. Often a very small minority suffices to resist in succession each part of the majority which does not know its own strength.

In spite of the differences of time and place, there are points of similarity in the histories of all nations fallen under the yoke. It is almost always after long civil troubles that tyranny establishes itself, because it offers to all exhausted and fearful parties the hope of finding protection in it. Bonaparte said of himself, with reason, that he knew marvelously well how to play upon the instrument of power. In fact, since he is attached to no principle and is restrained by no obstacle, he presents himself in the arena of circumstances like a supple and vigorous athlete, and at first glance knows what in each man and each association of men can serve his personal designs. His plan, to achieve the domination of France, was founded on three principal bases: to satisfy men's interests at the expense of their virtues, to deprave public opinion by sophistry, and to give the nation war as its objective in place of liberty. We shall see him follow these diverse routes with rare skill. The French, alas, only too eagerly seconded him; nevertheless, the blame must be placed on his melancholy genius; because, arbitrary governments having always prevented the nation from having fixed ideas on any subject, Bonaparte stirred up its passions without having to struggle against its principles. He then had it in his power to do honor to France and to establish himself firmly by respectable means; but distrust of the human race had completely dried up his soul, and he believed that there was nothing profound outside the region of evil.

We have already seen that General Bonaparte decreed a constitution in which there were no guarantees. Moreover, he took great care to preserve the laws issued during the Revolution in order that he might take whatever arms suited him from that detestable arsenal. The extraordinary commissions, the deportations, the exiles, the enslavement of the press, these measures unfortunately taken in the name of liberty, were very useful to tyranny. He justified their adoption sometimes by *raison d'état*, sometimes by the necessity of the times, sometimes by the activity of his adversaries, sometimes by the need to maintain tranquility. Such is the artillery of phrases by which absolute power is defended, because circumstances never have an end, and the more one wants to coerce by illegal measures, the more one creates discontents that justify the necessity of new acts of injustice. The establishment of liberty can result only from liberty itself.

One can arrive at a position of great power only by profiting from the tendency of one's century; Bonaparte carefully studied the spirit of his. There had been among the men of talent of the eighteenth century in France a superb enthusiasm for the principles that were the foundation of the happiness and dignity of mankind; but under the shelter of that great oak grew poisonous plants: egoism and mockery; and Bonaparte knew how to use these dismal propensities skillfully. He subjected to ridicule all glorious things save force, and proclaimed as the maxim of his reign, "Shame to the vanquished!" Accordingly one would be tempted to address to the disciples of his doctrine only one reproach, "And yet you have not succeeded," because all blame

based on feelings of morality would scarcely affect them.

It was necessary, however, to give a vital principle to this system of derision and immorality on which the civil government was founded. These negative forces did not suffice to sustain a forward motion without the impulsion of military successes. Order in the administration and in the finances, the embellishment of cities, the construction of canals and highways, in short, all that one can praise in internal affairs, had for its sole foundation the payments levied on foreigners. Nothing less than the revenues of the continent were necessary to obtain such advantages for France; and far from being based on durable institutions, the apparent grandeur of that colossus rested only on feet of clay. . . .

When at the close of the past century Bonaparte put himself at the head of the French people, the entire nation hoped for a free and constitutional government. The nobles, long outside France, aspired only to return peacefully to their homes; the Catholic clergy asked for tolerance; the republican warriors having eclipsed by their exploits the splendor of the distinctions of the nobility, the feudal race of the former conquerors respected the new victors, and the Revolution was made in men's minds. Europe was resigned to leaving to France the barrier of the Rhine and the Alps, and all that remained was to guarantee these possessions by curing the ills that their acquisition had brought in their train. But Bonaparte conceived the idea of effecting a counter-revolution which would work to his advantage by retaining in the state, so to speak, nothing new except himself. He reestablished the throne, the clergy, and the nobility; a monarchy, as Mr. Pitt said, without legitimacy and without limits; a clergy that was only the preacher of despotism; a nobility composed of old and new families but which performed no public function in the state and served only as an ornament to absolute power.

Bonaparte opened the door to old prejudices, flattering himself that he could stop them just short of his own omnipotence. It has often been said that if he had been moderate, he would have held his position. But what is meant by moderate? If he had established the English constitution in France sincerely and properly, without doubt he would still be Emperor. His victories made him a prince; his love of etiquette, his need of flattery, titles, decorations, and chamberlains made him appear again as an upstart. But however senseless was his system of conquest, once he became so miserable of soul as to see no greatness except in despotism, it was perhaps impossible for him to escape from continual wars; because in a country such as France what would a despot be without military glory? Could one oppress the nation at home without giving it at least the dismal compensation of dominating elsewhere in turn? The curse of the human race is absolute power, and all the French governments that succeeded the Constituent Assembly have perished because they yielded to this temptation under one pretext or another.

Revolutionary Emperor

ADOLPHE THIERS

Adolphe Thiers' (1797–1877) active role in the public life of France spans half a century. As a journalist and historian he contributed to the development of anti-Bourbon sentiment in the 1820's. He played a key role in the Revolution of 1830, sat in the Chamber of Deputies throughout the July Monarchy and was thrice a minister. Elected to the Constituent Assembly in 1848 and to the National Assembly the succeeding year, he went into exile after Louis-Napoleon's coup d'état of 1851, but he soon returned, and from 1863 to 1870 he once again sat in the parliament. In 1871 he was elected deputy in twenty-six departments, and became Chief of the Executive Power of the provisional government. His conversion to Republicanism alienated the monarchist majority in the National Assembly and led to his replacement in 1873. In the years when he was out of active politics—the '40's, '50's, and '60's—he produced a twenty-volume *Histoire du Consulate et de L'Empire*, which became the first great popular history of the Napoleonic years. Thiers, who as First Minister in 1840 had arranged for the ceremonial return of Napoleon's remains from Saint-Helena, was favorably inclined to Napoleon, but in the later volumes, written after the experience of living under a Second Empire, he became more critical. The selection printed here is taken from the eighteenth and twentieth volumes published in 1860 and 1862.

I N A FRANCE drained of blood, revolted by the spectacle that it had witnessed for ten years, General Bonaparte seized the dictatorship on the eighteenth of Brumaire, and that was not, whatever may be said about it, either a blunder or a crime. The dictatorship then was not a creation of servility, but a social necessity. To be possible,

From Adolphe Thiers, *Histoire du Consulate et de l'Empire* (Paris: Paulin, Lheureux et Cie., 1845–1862), XVII, 886–888, 897–899, XX, 723–730. [Editor's translation.]

liberty requires that government, parties, individuals allow themselves to be told everything with an unalterable patience. It is barely possible that they should be able to do so, when, having no serious reproach for one another, they find nothing to do but to slander one another. But when the men of the time could justly accuse each other of having killed, robbed, betrayed, negotiated with the foreign enemy, to imagine them face to face, peacefully discussing public affairs is a pure illusion. It is not for having taken the dictatorship that General Bonaparte must be called to account but for having used it as he did from 1800 to 1815.

When in the presence of the frightful disorders of a long revolution, his genius, intelligent as it was great, was applied to repair the mistakes of others, he left nothing to be desired. He had found the French embittered against each other, and he pacified the Vendée, recalled the *émigrés,* even restored to them a part of their lands. He had found the religious schism troubling all spirits; he did not pretend to be able to end it with his sword, he addressed himself respectfully to the spiritual head of the Catholic universe, whom he had reestablished on his throne, convinced him of the justice of his argument, led him to recognize the legitimate results of the French Revolution, obtained from him notably the consecration of the sale of the Church lands, the deposition of the old clergy, and the institution of an orthodox and new clergy, the absolution of juring priests or those who left their orders, and, after a negotiation of more than a year, a masterpiece of both shrewdness and patience, created out of all the relations of the State with the Church an admirable constitution, the only one of our constitutions that has survived, the Concordat. The Revolution had begun our civil laws under the inspiration of the most insane passions; he took them up again and completed them under the inspiration of good sense and the experience of centuries. He reimposed the necessary taxes, abolished to please the

multitude, organized an infallible accounting system, created an active, strong, and honest administration. Abroad, proud, resolute, but self-controlled, he knew how to make use of force while combining it with persuasion. In Switzerland he effected a second pacification of the Vendée, by means of an act of mediation, which under a different name, remains the definitive constitution of Switzerland. He reorganized Germany, convulsed by war, indemnifying the dispossessed princes with the lands of the Church and establishing a just equilibrium among the federated states. Thus holding the balance of German interests with an equitable and firm hand, and making it lean slightly in favor of Prussia without offending Austria, he prepared a Prussian alliance, the only one possible then and at the same time sufficient. After he had thus brought about the kind of commonweal that he deemed both practicable and desirable both at home and abroad, admired by the world, adored in France, nothing remained for him but to slumber in the bosom of that pure glory and to permit the tired world to slumber with him.

Vain dream! This man who had so well judged, so well curbed the passions of others, did not know how to restrain himself when his passions were hurt. . . .

If to obtain the true perspective on that extraordinary spectacle, we take a step backward as one does before an object too big to be judged close at hand, if we go back to the French Revolution itself, then all is explained, and we see that it is one of the phases of that immense revolution, a tragic and prodigious phase like the others, and we recognize in it that essential character of the imperial reign: intemperance. From 1789 to 1800 we witness the first outburst of the French Revolution; from 1800 to 1814 we witness its reaction upon itself, a reaction of which the Empire is the sovereign expression, and in both the one and the other the frenzy of passions are the essential trait. The French Revolution launches itself in the field of social reform, with its head full of generous sentiments, with its mind full of great and fruitful ideas, it encounters obstacles, is surprised by them, is annoyed by them, as if the carriage of humanity traveling on this earth ought not to experience friction, flies into a passion, becomes furious and drunk, sheds an abundance of human blood on the scaffold, shocks the world, and shocks itself by its own excesses, and out of that feeling is born a man, great like the Revolution, like it seeking the public welfare, wanting it ardently, immediately, and by all means, and then for its own good, it becomes necessary to make it itself retreat, to impose on it one denial after the other, one lesson after the other. Ah, if it were necessary to give lessons only to the French Revolution, Napoleon gives them to it admirably! He condemns regicide, the civil war, the religious schism, the captivity of the Pope, the universal republic, the fury of the war, and recalls the émigrés, restores the Pope to Rome, concludes the Concordat, grants Europe the peace of Lunéville and of Amiens. But the world is full of obstacles in whatever direction one moves, either forward or backward. At the first offence of his adversaries, worthy son of his mother, intemperate like her, tolerating neither resistance nor delay, the wise Consul flies into a passion, commits the regicide at Vincennes, reopens the schism, imprisons the Pope at Fontainebleau, falls again into war, this time general and continuous, substitutes the universal monarchy for the universal republic, and, phenomenon of unprecedented passion, like the Revolution, of which he is only the continuer, the representative, or the son, as some wish to call him, leaves behind him immense calamities, great principles, and a dazzling glory. The calamities and glory are for France, the principles for the entire world. . . .

Arrived at the government of France, which he found in real chaos, he felt even more than in Egypt and in Italy the need to reestablish order, calm, and prosperity. To give it a political constitution con-

cerned him the least. The friends of liberty (and we are in that number) reproach Napoleon for not having given it to France. While sharing their sentiments we believe that they are mistaken. With respect to politics, in fact, it was impossible that Napoleon become a definitive organizer, because our form of government was still to change many times under the wind of revolutions, and France, sometimes inclining toward power when it had just suffered from the agitations of liberty, sometimes inclining toward liberty when it had just suffered from an excess of power, France moved for three quarters of a century between despotism and anarchy, like a lamentably agitated pendulum, without settling, and without its being possible to say on what form it would finally stop, although in observing the course of events one can reasonably conclude that it will not be in despotism. He could not therefore, be the legislator of France with respect to politics, but he could be it, and he was, in all other respects.

On the morrow of the disorders of the Revolution the policy born of circumstances was not the policy of liberty but the policy of recovery. After bankruptcy, requisitions, confiscations, imprisonments, bloody executions, people wanted order in the finances, respect for persons and property, armies that were victorious but not reduced to pillage in order to exist, and finally rest and security. Napoleon, animated by the reparative spirit, was therefore acting — in the right tone — a part that coincided with the people's needs. Putting his hand to everything at once with a prodigious energy, he first remade the civil and criminal law, and the entire administration. When we say that he remade the law, we do not mean to claim, for example, that he invented the Civil Code. To pretend to invent in that style would be to pretend to invent human society, which comes not from yesterday but is as old as the appearance of man on our globe. There existed in France civil laws, some borrowed from Roman law, such as those that regulate contracts between

men, and which could not be changed from
century to century, from province to province; and the others drawn from national
customs and, like customs, essentially subject to change, such as those that regulate
the organizations of the family, conditions
of marriage, inheritances, etc. The first
should be reproduced in clear, precise style
— free of ambiguities that beget litigation.
The second ought to be modified following
the principles of true equality, which does
not insist that all men be equals in property,
in wealth, in honors, even if they are unequal in talents and in virtues, but which
wishes that they all be subject to the same
laws, subject to the same duties, punished
by the same punishments, paid the same
rewards, that the children of the same
father share equally in his estate, except
for the option left to that father to reward
the most worthy without disinheriting those
whom he wrongly does not love. On these
points, as on almost all, the French Revolution had oscillated from one extreme to
another according to the impulses to which
it was subjected. It was necessary to stop
at the proper point, between the retrogres-
sive tendencies and the foolishly innovating
tendencies in matters of marriage, inheritance, wills, etc. Napoleon had only the
education that it is possible to get in a good
military school but was born in the milieu
of the truths of 1789, and these truths,
which one may fail to recognize before they
have been disclosed, once known become
the light in whose glow all things are understood. Having MM. Portalis, Cambacérès, and especially Tronchet instruct
him each day on the business that the
Council of State would take up the next
day, he thought about it for twenty-four
hours, listened to the discussion, then with
a matchless good sense, fixed exactly the
point where it was necessary to stop between the old order and the new order, and
what is more, with his power of concentration forced everyone to work. He contributed thus in two decisive ways to the
making of our codes, in determining the
degree of innovation and in pushing the

work to completion. Several times before
him that work had been undertaken, and
each time ceding to the pressure of the day
they had allowed themselves to be carried
away on the spur of the moment, then had
indulged in exaggerations that had soon left
them ashamed and sorry, after which they
had abandoned the work. Napoleon took
that vessel grounded on the shore, floated
it, and propelled it to port. That ship was
the Civil Code, and no one can deny that
that code is the code of the modern civilized
world. It is certainly for a military man a
beautiful and pure glory to have merited
the attachment of his name to the organization of modern civil society, and it is equally
a beautiful merit for France, where the
work was accomplished! It can be said in
fact that if England had the merit to con-
tribute the best political form of modern
states, France had that of contributing by
the Civil Code the best form of the social
state — a beautiful and noble sharing of
glory between the two most civilized nations of the globe!

While Napoleon was thus occupied with
civil legislation, he also applied his expedit-
ing and creative hand to the administration.
Finding the administration of the provinces
in the same state as the other parts of the
government, he turned, as he had done
with civil law, this part of past notions into
present exaggerations, and, borrowing valid
elements here and there, he created the
modern administration. The past exhibited
provincial estates administering themselves
and enjoying, insofar as local interests were
concerned, almost complete powers. As
long as the state's subsidies were assured,
the monarchy let the provinces do what
they wished, either by a survival of respect
for the old treaties of union or because it
had the confused idea that since it granted
no liberty at the center, it ought to leave
much to the extremities. The monarchy
thus gave itself full power concerning general affairs, and abandoned to the country
the regulation of local affairs. That tacit
contract was to fall before the great phenomenon of the French Revolution. It was

neither proper that the monarchy should be all-powerful on the great destinies of the country, nor that the provinces should be all-powerful on local affairs, because the destiny of the country ought to be restored to the will of the country itself, and provincial interests to its control. These riches, which the provinces dispose of in decreeing their expenses, are a part of the general wealth, which they should not dissipate carelessly; these local regulations that the communes establish for themselves, touching on industry, on markets, on the nature of taxes, are a part of social legislation that they should not be permitted to establish according to their private views.

The great phenomenon of modern unity ought to consist in this, that the monarchy would give up its total power over general matters, the provinces would, as far as they were concerned, give up their total power over private matters, that they should mutually interpenetrate in some fashion, and merge into a powerful unit, directed by the common intelligence of the nation. From that moment there should be at the center of the state a chief of the executive power surrounded by the principal citizens of France to deal with general affairs, and in the departments the administrative chiefs surrounded by notable citizens of the locality for private affairs, but themselves subordinate concerning government matters to the authority of the government, and concerning department matters to the supervision of the government. Hence the prefect and the departmental council. If circumstances had permitted the First Consul to be consistent, he should have made the departmental councils elective. But on the morrow of the frightful convulsions that had just been experienced, between the madmen of 1793, odious to the country, and the big proprietors returning from the emigration, elections would have been impossible, or at least subject to great inconvenience. He reserved to himself the choosing of wise, moderate men who could administer tolerably well. It was a consequence of his dictatorship, which was to be

transient and would disappear with him. Nevertheless, the principle was established, that of a chief or prefect administering under the control of a council, intended to be elective when our terrible divisions were sufficiently healed.

But state surveillance over the level of expenditures, the system of taxes, and the nature of regulations had to be exercised, and it could not be delegated without guarantees to the executive power, representative of the state. Napoleon made use of an institution that Sieyès had furnished him by borrowing from the former monarchy. The Royal Council, among other matters with which it was formerly occupied, gave its advice on affairs that grew out of relations of the state with the provinces. These relations, having become closer under the new regime, were to devolve naturally on the Council of State. Napoleon, without proceeding theoretically, but making use of what he had at hand for the accomplishment of his plans, made the Council of State the repository of that superior surveillance, which constitutes essentially what is called centralization. Desiring that the budgets of the communes and of the departments be controlled by the state, that their rules be brought back to the principles of 1789, that this commune not be permitted to reestablish guilds, that another not be permitted to levy taxes contrary to modern doctrines, that conflicts among them have an arbiter, he confided these diverse matters to the Council of State, presiding over it himself with indefatigable persistence and application. Without that regulator, our civilization would become the most intolerable of despotisms. But counsel of prudence in matters of communal expenditures, mediator in matters of one commune complaining against another, finally legislator in matters of municipal regulations, the Council of State is an enlightened, firm regulator, and even independent, although appointed by the executive power, because in its functions it draws on an administrative spirit that prevails over the spirit of servility, and which, under all regimes, after a momentary docility toward the new government, rises again almost voluntarily, and reappears like a vigorous vegetable whose branches resume their growth after a momentary disturbance.

It was in presiding assiduously over that council, when he was not in the field, and presiding seven or eight hours at a stretch, with a strength of concentration, a rightness of rare good sense, and respect for the opinion of others that he always observed in specialized matters, that, sometimes ruling on fact, sometimes imagining and modifying according to the need of our administrative laws, thus creating at once legislation and jurisprudence, he became

the very author of that administration, firm, active, honest, which made our financial accounts the clearest ever known, our power the most stable in Europe, and which, when our governments fall into folly under the influence of revolutions, alone does not follow suit, conducts the current affairs of the country wisely and consistently . . . keeps France erect while the head of France wavers. . . . Thus war in rendering him irresistible made Napoleon a bad politician, but on the other hand it made him one of the greatest organizers who has appeared in the world, and there as in all things he has been the double product of nature and of events.

New Roman Emperor

EDGAR QUINET

Edgar Quinet (1803–1875), Professor of Literature in the Collège de France, was known for his books on religious history and on German and Italian culture, but he attracted special attention to himself by his lectures on the Jesuits, on Christianity and the French Revolution, and on other religious subjects, which led, in 1846, to the suspension of his courses. He was elected to the Constituent Assembly in 1848, and twenty-three years later, in the election of 1871, he again became a deputy. The intervening years, beginning in 1851, he spent in exile in Belgium and Switzerland. They were years of bitter hostility to Napoleon III and the Second Empire, and that hostility carried over to his writing of La Révolution, published in 1865, and is reflected in his judgment in that volume of the first Napoleon.

NAPOLEON claimed that in 1802 he was free to choose between Catholicism and Protestantism, that the nation would have blindly followed him in the choice he might make. We have just seen the contrary; France was already bound. Let us add that Catholicism alone fit the plan and the logic of General Bonaparte's

design; if he had pushed France to profound innovations in religion, he would have been in contradiction with and revolt against himself.

Go down to the base of his thought, you will see that his idea was the empire of Constantine and of Theodosius; he inherited that tradition from his ancestors like

From Edgar Quinet, La Révolution (Paris: A. Lacroix, Verboeckhoven et Cie., 2d edition, 1865), II, 529–541. [Editor's translation.]

all the Italian Ghibellines. I have already shown elsewhere that it was a social instinct that he bore from birth. Instead of offering the religious emancipation of the individual conscience, he always pictured the kind of pope to whom he would have been the emperor and the master; a conception that is nothing other than the idea of the Ghibellines and of the Glossarists of the Middle Ages. From that mixture of Italian genius and French genius was formed that extraordinary logic by which he so easily forced France even into the political institutions of Charlemagne.

He who brings this new element to the study of Napoleon will see what was formerly strangest in his projects illuminated by an unexpected light. All that is in the Ghibelline, Latin, Byzantine tradition reappears in Napoleon, and everything that is lacking in Napoleon is also lacking in the Ghibelline tradition of political and religious power. When he dreams of his future, it is always of the obedient world of a Theodosius, of a Justinian such as the imperial administration of the Middle Ages represented him. As for modern liberty, it was worse than an anachronism amid such conceptions; it would appear to him only as a popular caprice and a trap for his power.

That man, so profoundly modern in so many respects and who became in so many others a prince of the Middle Ages, a Carolingian (and that is too early to stop, one must go back to Byzantium); that Caesar who is at the same time Charlemagne, antique and feudal; that procession of dukes, of counts, of barons, issue of a leveling revolution — there are so many enigmas that baffle the world, impossible to decipher if one stops at the surface. These same contradictions are clarified, explained, and flooded with light if, conforming to the spirit of our times that brings the influence of race into every question, you will discover in Napoleon the transmission of native characters that his imperial ancestors of Florence left him. In many respects, by his Caesarian superstition of the *Monarchia*

del mondo, he is unknowingly the executor of the chimerical plans of Dante, which he did not read; he became the contemporary of them. Can one expect Dante in the fourteenth century to have the ideas of the French Revolution?

In the place of Napoleon put for a moment, as many men wished, Moreau, Hoche, Joubert, or Bernadotte; and ponder the difference, not only of genius but of nature. None of these men of pure French race would have found in the archives of his family the innate tradition of the Roman universal monarchy. Would Hoche or Joubert have had at birth both the vision of a grand empire, without frontier, without limit, that would not even consent to be bound by the ocean? None of them obviously would have found that conception, more extraordinary than grand, of Napoleon. Italian blood flowing from vein to vein, from the partisans of Frederick Barbarossa and of Henry VII to the Bonaparte Ghibelline of the sixteenth century alone could produce that colossus of glory and vertigo that will surprise us, dizzy us, worry us until, at last, we come to see and understand the historical reason for it.

In triumphantly restoring Catholicism Napoleon, it is now certain, provided the necessary base for his authority. That which he took by surprise on the 18 Brumaire he consecrated by the Concordat. After having subjugated men's wills by force, he made them tractable by religion. All that comes from a single thought.

The theologians were amazed by the sureness of the young general's view in religious matter. I readily believe it. From the first glance he had perfectly understood that Catholicism was a necessary part of authority as he conceived it; only there did he find the discipline of mind that he wanted to make the rule of the political order. The Concordat was his visit to the sands of Jupiter Ammon.

It would have been a mortal contradiction for him to help men win individual liberty of conscience when he planned to subjugate them to his sole will. If he had pushed France to Protestantism, he would have dated his power from the sixteenth century and not, as he intended, from the era of the Caesars. A Ghibelline and Protestant emperor is repugnant to the nature of things.

In that potent seizure of absolute power, it must never be said he made a mistake. One point eluded him. This was the so-called liberties of the Gallican Church. Here his genius lacked penetration: He did not see that these liberties that he wished to turn into bonds had perished like all the others. He committed himself to that frail surface which broke under his feet, as will happen to all who imitate him on this point. He intended to harness the Church to his chariot by the four articles of Bossuet, which the Church no longer wanted; these articles, which limited the power of the Papacy, were only a snare. He quickly perceived this.

This was the weak side of the Empire. To bring the earth again under the rule of Constantine or of Theodosius, what was necessary? First to restore the Papacy along with Catholicism, then to substitute himself for the former; the Pope would have been only a patriarch in the hand of the Emperor. Napoleon would preside, like Constantine, over the councils of Nicea. He would have possessed absolute power over souls as well as over bodies.

Such was the goal. He lacked the means to attain it because he depended upon the Gallican Church, which was only a shadow. There for the first time he mistook appearance for reality. On the one hand he wished to make no change in dogma; on the other he wanted to return the church violently to the state of dependence in which it was in the third century. In that path, having none of the audacity of spirit of an innovator or of a reformer, he encountered anathema and excommunication, which stopped him short.

From that moment his edifice lacked a foundation, and he could not find another for it. To return the world to the age of Constantine, it was necessary to drive po-

litical society and religious society back to the third century. Napoleon could achieve only the first. The Church, in remaining rooted in the Middle Ages and theocratic papacy, barred his route and prevented his return to the Byzantine ideal.

Not being able to depend upon Rome or Byzantium or upon the modern world, he found that his structure rested only on himself alone and that it would stand or fall with him. Basically he sought two contradictory things: the one, that the Pope remain the chief of Catholicism; the other, that he become the chief of the Pope. When the tiara was on the ground, he dared not pick it up and put it on his head. That man of such audacity in the affairs of this world, if he had shown an equal temerity in the things of the spirit, would no longer represent the genius of the Latin tradition.

Already the unfathomable image of Napoleon escapes us; we alter it, we change it at the mercy of our mellowed thoughts. In spite of us, the fable is formed; develops under our eyes. In the poems of the Middle Ages Attila is no longer the scourge of God; he becomes a melancholy knight errant, who went praying from monastery to monastery. Charlemagne is no longer the conqueror and the baptizer of the Saxons in a river of blood; he is always crying in his beard among his peers. By such a transformation will Napoleon become the representative and the compliant precursor of the era of representative governments? Let us leave to Attila his scourge, to Charlemagne his capitularies, to Napoleon his decrees. Let us not confuse history with poetry.

You saw the French Revolution break out to free France from the yoke of the Byzantine and Roman tradition under the double form of political and religious power. In 1802 the chaos clears up, we begin to see the light, examine the denouement. That very tradition that was thought to be dissolved is reestablished; that very yoke that was believed broken is repaired under another name; and this is what the First Consul calls "to consolidate definitively the results of the Revolution." Something much more extraordinary, the sophistry of the ambition of a great captain becomes the judgment of the historian and the snare of a part of posterity. . . .

There have been two great conquests that left their imprint on us: the one by the Romans, the other by the Franks. The French Revolution freed the nation from the conquest of the Franks; that of the Romans still persists.

The French Revolution having miscarried on the two principal points, religion and politics, one result was that the French genius was not able to emancipate itself from Rome, that from these two points of view, the mass of the nation, the Gauls, remained captives and serfs of the Romans, in the form of Caesar and the sovereign pontiff. What continued to reign over the Gauls was the Caesarian tradition through the Emperor and the Pope.

Coming on the scene at that moment, you see France, just emerged from absolute rule, return into it with big strides, and the ring of iron that one had believed broken was again closed.

Between its Tarquins and its Caesar France had known only a few years of a tumultuous Republic.

Between 1792 and 1804 the French experienced all the political stages that the Romans took centuries to pass through between the epoch of the Tarquins and the epoch of the Caesars.

That vast extent of Roman history, those transformations, those absolute differences of customs, of laws, of regimes have with us been compressed into twelve years. The same men have witnessed in France while still in their youth the old Tarquins in the *ancien régime* before 1789, and the Republic of the Gracchi in that of Saint-Just, and the empire of Justinian in that of Napoleon. . . .

The French in 1789 had encountered three great obstacles that they proposed to overcome: the absolute power, the Catholicism of Rome, and administrative centralization. The storm once passed, at the beginning of the century, you see these three great obstacles reappear and rise again to their full height: the absolute power with the First Consul, Roman Catholicism by the Concordat, the centralization by the new administration. The Latin spirit of an aging Rome is found again everywhere. The old river after having crossed the lake and having deposited some of its sediment, reappeared at the other end and resumed its former character.

A highly developed civil law and no political law or only the illusion of one, such was the character of the world of Byzantium; you discover with surprise that the same character still survives after eighteen centuries among the first Latin people.

The French after 1804 believed that they had saved the Revolution because they had the five codes; they reasoned like the Byzantines, who also believed that they had saved Athens and Rome and the heroic soul of civilization, because Justinian had granted them the Digest and the Pandects.

The ancients left to conquered peoples their civil laws, knowing very well that sovereignty does not reside there. Who would have thought the Revolution would keep only that which conquerors grant to the vanquished?

You would never have guessed that after so many immortal days the French would retain only that which no one disputed them, private law.

In reality, what did, then, remain of the political Revolution? An ideal, a flag, some words of justice that drift on the deep and on which the eyes of the human race are fixed. Never a greater shipwreck nor more radiant wreckage. Three words left as heritage to the world and millions of men dead in vain for them, that, too, is sublime.

Do not compare, furthermore, the repression of the human spirit under Napoleon with that of the late Empire. In the latter a municipal life survived everywhere, which permitted people to breathe; you would find not the shadow of this in the regime established in 1800.

Are there stunted revolutions as there are stunted growths in vegetable and animal organisms?

At the beginning of the century the Revolution is a monument half in ruins on prodigious foundations, demolished in a few days by the hand of a conqueror; but in its immense foundations that Babel still reveals here and there the plan that posterity will complete if it knows how to profit from experiences accumulated here and sterile up to the present.

After the gigantic effort of 1789 to 1800 what do you see? A strange idea, Italian, Ghibelline, that of the world empire invading, dominating everything, this idea settles itself on top of the world to rule it. The French Revolution, incomplete, stops with its work half finished, having been unable to find its form. Napoleon occupied that enormous void and filled it with his name.

If a people has allowed itself to become shallow, it becomes inevitably the prey of force and of chance.

Napoleon, at Saint-Helena, made his apology in making that of Caesar. The crossing of the Rubicon reminds him of the 18 Brumaire; he seeks to persuade himself, and he does persuade himself, in fact, that after having overturned all the laws Caesar was above reproach, because he had retained all the exterior forms and even the names, Senate, consuls, Tribune. Was he hoping thus to deceive himself? No, he had no need of that. But he wanted through the complicity of history to consecrate the sophistry that men had accepted from his mouth.

Strange conspiracy of these sovereign sophists who transmit from one to the other across the centuries the same royal cunning! Would they were content to dominate the world! The misfortune is that they also want its approval. It does not suffice for them that their subjects be submissive, they want them to be convinced. It is not enough that one bend the knee if the intelligence does not bend in its turn.

Alexander is not content to rule over the Greek world; it is necessary that he be adored as the son of Jupiter Ammon. From that moment men began to worship men: first catastrophe of antiquity.

Caesar is not content to be master of the Roman world; he wanted also to be regarded as the liberator of men. Since that time the Caesarian fallacy blinds the earth, to the complete debilitation of the antique world.

In the same way Napoleon is not content to put the world at his feet; he wishes, too, that his absolute domination and the silence that accompanies it be the advent of modern liberty and that he be the faithful and legitimate son, not of Jupiter Ammon, but of the Revolution. . . .

Caesar and Napoleon both wanted the same thing, absolute power. But the means that they employed were different. Caesar did not think of restoring the institutions of the past because those institutions were free. Napoleon, on the contrary, returned by his imitation of Charlemagne, to the Middle Ages, because behind him in the past he had despotism.

Man of the Revolution

ALPHONSE AULARD

At a time when most of the writing on Napoleon was still polemical Alphonse Aulard (1849–1928) was establishing the "scientific" study of the French Revolution. He first attracted attention in the mid-'80's by the publication of three volumes on parliamentary eloquence during the Revolution, and in 1887 he was called to the new chair of French Revolutionary history founded at the Sorbonne by the city of Paris, which he occupied until 1922. In 1887 he founded and for many years edited La Révolution française, the first scholarly journal devoted to the study of the Revolution, and he edited and published weighty collections of documents on the Jacobin society, the Committee of Public Safety, and Paris under the Consulate. He is known chiefly, however, for his classic Histoire politique de la Révolution, published in 1901. In it he carries his story up to the establishment of the Empire in 1804. He professed to write only objective history, but his judgments of the Revolution and Napoleon reflected his political sympathies as an active member of the Radical Party.

THE THREE consuls designated by the new constitution began to sit on 4 Nivôse, Year VIII (December 25, 1799), that is, forty-four days before it was known if the people had accepted that constitution. Beginning with that first meeting, the tentative procedures of the provisional Consulate were at an end; the actions of Bonaparte swept his colleagues into a whirlwind of activity. On that day of 4 Nivôse, there were both notable words and acts. A proclamation of the First Consul to the French people inaugurated a new order of things: governmental stability, a strong army, order, justice, moderation — these are the words that were substituted for the language and for the principles of the Revolution. . . .

The Council of State had been created and organized since the preceding day, 3 Nivôse. Charged with drawing up the projected laws and the regulations of public administration, that council prepared the decisions of the consuls on all matters of litigation. It also decided if a functionary was to be brought before the courts. It had the vague and redoubtable power to "develop the sense of the laws" on request of the consuls. It is there that Bonaparte organized his government, his policy, his reign, presiding, haranguing, winning the councilors to his ideas by persuasion before the victory of Marengo had made him a despot, thereafter subjugating them and tyrannizing them by the expression, often brutal, of his will. . . . On 4 Nivôse at four o'clock this council was installed and immediately expressed the opinion that the constitution had implicitly abrogated the laws that excluded ex-nobles and relatives of émigrés from public office. This was a very grave matter: Bonaparte showed that if necessary he would legislate through the Council of State without the assistance of the Tribunate and of the Legislative Body.

In conformity with the Constitution, Sieyès, Roger Ducos, Cambacérès, and Le Brun had appointed the citizens who would form the majority of the Senat Conservateur. Their choice fell on distinguished

From Alphonse Aulard, Histoire politique de la Révolution française (Paris: Armand Colin, 1901), pp. 712–720, 758–760, 778–780, 783. Reprinted by permission of Librairie Armand Colin. [Editor's translation.]

17

men almost all of whom had deserved well of the Revolution, like Monge, Volney, Garat, Garran-Coulon, Kellermann, Cabanis. Sieyès and Roger Ducos entered the Senate *ex officio,* and it was immediately increased by co-optation until the constitutional number of sixty members had been attained. . . .

The Senate at once appointed the 300 members of the Legislative Body and the 100 members of the Tribunate, and it did not make these appointments in a narrow or servile spirit. On the contrary, it made up the Legislative Body almost entirely of the elite of former members of the various revolutionary assemblies with a marked preference for men of 1789, but without excluding ardent republicans like Grégoire, Bréard, Florent Guiot, or even the personal adversaries of Napoleon. . . .

The Tribunate was composed of men whose characters and whose pasts fitted them for the role of constitutional opposition for which that assembly seemed created. . . .

The Tribunate and the Legislative Body fulfilled with firmness and intelligence their duty of opposing nascent despotism and rejected several proposed illiberal laws. But these assemblies, so distinguished in their membership, did not constitute a national representation; they did not even represent the notables, for whom the lists were not to be drawn up until the Year IX. Thus their opposition was sterile and impotent; Bonaparte would have little trouble in breaking it.

During the provisional Consulate the periodical press had enjoyed more liberty perhaps than it had ever had since June 2, 1793. Thus, in the *Moniteur* of 29 Brumaire, Year VIII, in forms at once respectful and hypothetical, public opinion was warned against the ambition of Bonaparte, and at the same time he was advised, in case peace was not made in three months, to "divest himself of the civil power" and go to put himself at the head of an army. The *Bien-Informée,* in its number of 14 to 24 Frimaire, openly decried the illiberal

constitutional projects, and contrasted them with the American constitution, which it reprinted. One reads in the *Gazette de France* of 26 Frimaire: "The constitution was proclaimed on the twenty-fourth in all the *arrondissements* of Paris. Here is an anecdote that will reveal the spirit of the Parisians. A member of the municipal guard read the constitution, and everyone was struggling so hard to hear the reading that no one heard two consecutive phrases. A woman said to her neighbor: 'I heard nothing.' 'Why, I didn't miss a word.' 'Well! What is there in the constitution?' 'There is Bonaparte.'" It is through these epigrammatic anecdotes that the opposition of some journals manifested itself. Bonaparte feared that, associated with the opposition of the Tribunate and the Legislative Body, it would prevent his becoming the master. On 27 Nivôse, Year VIII, "considering that a portion of the journals that are printed in the Department of the Seine are instruments in the hands of the enemies of the Republic," he issued an order to suppress all the political journals of Paris except thirteen. . . .

Without doubt the elite of the Parisian press was maintained, even the opposition *Gazette de France.* But the *Moniteur,* then the most important of the journals, had become official since the 7 Nivôse, and the twelve others were threatened with immediate suppression if they inserted "articles disrespectful of the social compact, of the sovereignty of the people and of the glory of the armies," or if they published "invectives against governments and nations friendly or allied with the Republic, even if these articles were taken from foreign periodicals." In sum, all opposition whatsoever was forbidden to the press, and one can almost say that from the order of 27 Nivôse, Year VIII, dates the beginning of despotism.

Presented as a provisional measure "for the duration of the war," that suspension of the liberty of the press did not stop with the Peace of Amiens, and lasted throughout the Consulate and the Empire. . . .

The political journals of the provinces were not affected by the order of 27 Nivôse. But those that exhibited any independence were suppressed by individual measures. . . . As for foreign journals, entry into France was forbidden to almost all, except during the first weeks after the peace of Amiens. . . .

Nevertheless, it should not be assumed that at the end of the Consulate all the press was absolutely domesticated. After the murder of the Duc d'Enghien the *Journal des Débats* dared to reveal its disapproval by publishing a translation of a speech by which Pacuvius, in *Silius Italicus,* turns his son from the plan to assassinate Hannibal. Suard, asked to write an apology for that murder in the *Publiciste,* wrote a proud letter of refusal.

Once the Empire is established, the vestiges of independence will disappear and the political press will belong completely to the government.

Despotism was already to be found in the constitution of the Year VIII, but implicit and half-hidden under formulas that were by Bonaparte's wish short and obscure, as he later declared in referring to the Italian constitution. The very day that he was certain that the nation had accepted the constitution, the mask fell, and the First Consul presented to the Tribunate and to the Legislative Body the project of law (which became the Law of 28 Pluviôse, Year VIII) on administrative reorganization, a project that established an absolute centralization for the benefit of one man, and by which all right of election of officials whatsoever was withdrawn from the people (who retained scarcely anything of their former sovereignty save the right to elect directly the justices of the peace.)

The constitution had declared that the territory of the republic was divided into departments and into communal arrondissements. The division into departments was retained, with no change other than the suppression of the Department of the Mont-Terrible, which was combined with that of the Haut-Rhin. As for the communal arrondissements, which the consti-

tution had named without defining them, one could assume that they were a continuation of those cantonal municipalities by which the authors of the constitution of the Year III had tried to establish a real communal life. But it was precisely these communes, strong enough to have a life and action of their own, that might have raised an obstacle to despotic centralization. All the municipalities were reestablished as the Constitutent had formerly established them, and as we have them still, that is to say there was a return to a sterilizing dispersion of municipal life.

Under the name of arrondissements, the districts, abolished by the constitution of the Year III, were reestablished, but their number was reduced. As for the administrators, the constitution had made it clear that they would be appointed by the executive power, but not that the administration would be confined, in the departments and in the arrondissements, to a single man. The Law of 28 Pluviôse, Article 3, provided that "the prefect alone will be entrusted with the administration." He had in each arrondissement a sub-prefect under his orders. This was the resurrection of the intendants and their sub-delegates, but much stronger than under the *ancien régime* because they could not be opposed by any body, any institution, any tradition.

The preamble posed the principle "that *to administrate* ought to be the task of one man; *to judge* the task of several." There are two kinds of judgments: 1st the judgments that consist of apportioning taxes; they were confided to general councils, to arrondissement councils, and to municipal assessors; 2d judgments of litigious matters; they were confided to prefectoral councils.

Appointed for three years, the general councils and the arrondissement councils sit only fifteen days yearly, for the apportionment of direct taxes among the arrondissements and among the communes. The general council also votes, for the expenses of the department, *centimes additionnels,* which the prefect uses as he sees fit on condition of rendering an annual account to the general council, which will confine itself to "hearing" that report and to expressing its opinion on the needs of the department.

The prerogatives of the municipal councils are a little more extensive; they can hear and debate the account of receipts and expenditures that will be submitted by the mayor to the sub-prefect, who will give it its definitive form; they deliberate on loans, the *octrois,* etc. Civil affairs as well as the police are confided to mayors and their assistants. But, in cities of more than 20,000 inhabitants, the police are in the hands of the central government. In Paris the regime is unique with a Prefect of Police. Prefects, sub-prefects, members of general councils and of arrondissement councils, mayors, assistants, municipal councilors are appointed, some by the First Consul, the others by the prefects. As for the *tribunal contentieux* established in each department under the name of the prefectoral council, and composed, according to the department, of five, four, or three members, its members are appointed by the First Consul, and that tribunal can be presided over by the prefect, who, in case of a tie, has the deciding vote. Thus after having distinguished between administration and judgment, the framers of the law, in the interests of despotism, confuse administration and judgment. . . .

Thus was organized the despotic centralization; but at first one saw only the happy consequences because of Bonaparte's skillful choice of prefects and of sub-prefects, and because at the beginning he could, through them, rapidly achieve the improvements of all kinds that his genius inspired in him. The administration was rapid, simple. It was found to be equitable. Europe appeared to "envy us." Only gradually did it become brutal and tyrannical, in proportion as the master himself was transformed from a good despot into a bad despot.

That transformation was slow, and the various phases were ill-understood by contemporaries. At the time of the vote of the constitution of the Year VIII, Bonaparte retained a kind of republican simplicity. It was only on the 30 Pluviôse that he moved into the Tuileries, as a law authorized him to do. There was not yet a consular court; at first Bonaparte surrounded himself with a court of heroic statues. He ordered that the great gallery of the Tuileries be decorated with statues of Demosthenes, Alexander, Hannibal, Scipio, Brutus, Cicero, Caesar, Turenne, Condé, Washington, Frederick, Mirabeau, Marceau, etc. He retained a part of republican etiquette, and the title of citizen alone remained in use. On the news of the death of Washington, an order of the day (18 Pluviôse, Year VIII) prescribed a period of mourning in the name of the ideas of liberty and equality.

But, side by side with these republican usages, new manners, or rather old manners, timidly reappeared. The opera balls, forbidden since 1790, reopened; people here disguised themselves as monks, as councilors of Parlement as much in reaction as in parody. A brilliant reception given by Talleyrand on the 6 Ventôse, Year VIII (February 25, 1800) revealed the intention of the First Consul to rally around him the personnel of the old regime and that of the new; one saw here MM. de Coigny, Dumas, Portalis, Ségur l'ainé, La Rochefoucauld-Liancourt, De Crillon, Mmes. de Vergennes, de Castellane, d'Aiguillon, de Noailles. At the time of the coup d'état of 18 Brumaire and during the provisional Consulate, Bonaparte had surrounded himself almost exclusively with men of 1789, liberals, members of the Institute. He began now to procure new elements to form his future court, and he sought them from the *ancien régime.* As for the liberals who took seriously their roles as tribunes or legislators and who were already forming an opposition, he was out of humor with them and already branded them with the name of *idéologues.*

Soon he was going to alter again that French patriotism whose decline had facilitated the success of the coup d'état of 18

Brumaire. The man of the Revolution had the habit of associating the word virtue with the word patriotism. In place of the word virtue Bonaparte began to use the word honor. Thus on 17 Ventôse, Year VIII, it is "in the name of honor" that he summons the conscripts to join their units before the following 15 Germinal. The new patriotism is a rivalry among Frenchmen for a goal fixed by Bonaparte. Honor is the glory of having been proclaimed by Bonaparte victor in that rivalry. It is precisely that honor in which Montesquieu had seen the mainspring of monarchies, and it is precisely a return to the monarchical spirit, a changing of citizens into subjects that Bonaparte prepares by that substitution of the word honor for the words virtue, liberty, equality with which the Revolution had loved to embellish patriotism. It is no longer a matter of loving the country for its own sake; men are going to become accustomed to loving it for the sake of a master, to love it in a master as in the time of the *ancien régime*. . . .

Beginning with the Life Consulate Bonaparte abandoned the attitude of president of the republic in the American manner that he had until then approximately retained. In the *senatus-consulte* that proclaimed him consul for life, it was no longer "Citizen Bonaparte" but "Napoleon Bonaparte." Thus emerged from the shadows that given name of sonorous syllables that was going to become the name of the Emperor. The silly adulation had begun; in its number of 23 Floréal, Year X, the *Journal des défenseurs de la patrie* inserted an alleged "extract from a German journal" in which it was stated that the word Napoleon, according to its Greek root, meant Valley of the Lion. A circular from the minister of the interior of 16 Thermidor, Year X, invited the prefects to celebrate 27 Thermidor (August 15), the anniversary of the birth of the First Consul and of the ratification of the Concordat by the Pope. On that day there were splendid illuminations in Paris, and everywhere appeared the initials N.B. . . .

Soon Bonaparte had himself granted a civil list of 6,000,000, which the minister of finance Gaudin introduced in the budget of the Year XI (in place of the 500,000 francs that the constitution of the Year VIII had granted to the first consul).

Since Marengo, and especially since the peace, the quarters of Bonaparte at the Tuileries, simple at first, had become luxurious, almost royal. There was a governor of the palace, Duroc, and prefects of the palace. . . . Four ladies were attached to the person of Madame Bonaparte. . . . All military and crude at the outset, that court was transformed under the influence of Josephine, and also by the will of Bonaparte, who desired that his entourage be neither entirely military nor entirely civil. At first the French coat with saber and boots was worn, which made people smile. At the celebration of July 14, 1802, Napoleon appeared in a coat of red Lyon silk, without ruffles and with a black cravat. After the establishment of the Life Consulate the sword and silk stockings replaced the saber and the boots. The questions of dress became a serious matter. To have a hair-bag and to powder one's hair was a way of paying court to the First Consul, as did the minister of finance, Gaudin. Bonaparte did not powder his hair but wore it as before; but he encouraged these futilities, these mimicries of the *ancien régime*, and all that could transform his functionaries and his generals into courtiers divided among themselves and occupied with trifles. The character of this new court and that which especially distinguished it from the old is that although women ornamented it, they exercised almost no political influence in it, or they were only instruments of the policy of Bonaparte, who, in his palace as in France, remained the master.

Of all the acts of the Consulate, that in which contemporaries especially saw a return to the manners of the monarchy was the Law of 29 Floréal, Year X (May 19, 1802), which created a Legion of Honor, "in execution of Article 87 of the constitution, concerning military rewards, and also to reward civil services and virtues." That Legion, of which the First Consul was the chief, was composed of a Grand Council of Administration and fifteen cohorts (each of which would have its own chief), each including seven *grands officiers* with salaries of 5000 francs, twenty *commandants* with salaries of 2000 francs, thirty *officiers* with salaries of 1000 francs, and 350 *légionnaires* with salaries of 250 francs, all appointed for life. . . . Named by the Grand Council of Administration, over which presided the First Consul, the members of the Legion of Honor were chosen from among military men who had "rendered major services for the state in the war of liberty.". . . and among "the citizens who, by their knowledge, their talents, their virtues contributed to the establishment or the defense of the principles of the Republic, or who contributed to making justice or public administration liked and respected." Each individual admitted into the Legion of Honor had "to swear on his honor to devote himself to the service of the Republic, to the preservation of its territory in its integrity, to the defense of its government, of its laws and of the rights they sanction; to combat by all means authorized by justice, reason, and law all enterprise tending to reestablish the feudal regime, to revive the titles and ranks that were attributed of it; finally, to cooperate with all his power in the maintenance of liberty and equality."

Despite these republican formulas, the proposal to establish the Legion of Honor encountered lively opposition in the Council of State. . . . Orators of the Tribunate criticized it bitterly as counter-revolutionary. It was adopted by that assembly by a majority of only 56 votes against 38, and in the Legislative Body by a majority of 170 votes against 110. At first decried and ridiculed for being a civil institution, the Legion of Honor was soon accepted by opinion, and its insignia were so sought after that it was a powerful instrument for the personal ambition of Bonaparte. . . .

It has been seen that it was the government of the Republic that was entrusted to an emperor, and, in the formula of promulgation of the law, Napoleon had to style himself Emperor "by the grace of God and the constitutions of the Republic." What ought to be understood by that word Republic? On 10 Frimaire, Year XIII, the President of the Senate, François (de Neufchateau), in congratulating the Emperor on the results of the plebiscite on heredity, said that that result "brought the vessel of the Republic into port." And he declared: "Yes, Sire, of the Republic! That word can offend an ordinary monarch. Here the word is proper before him whose genius has made us enjoy it in the way such a Republic may exist in a great people." To wish to establish the "pure republic" the "republic strictly speaking," that is, democracy, is to prepare "fetters for the future"; because, in the state of ignorance in which the mass of people exist, liberty and democracy are as irreconcilable as the genius of Napoleon would be impotent to reconcile them. François (de Neufchateau) wanted to put the advantages of the monarchy in the Republic . . . and, commenting on the Emperor's oath, he found in it all the guarantees of a "representative state." Napoleon replied with the brevity of a despot: "I mount the throne to which I am called by the unanimous wishes of the Senate, of the people, and of the army, my heart filled with the consciousness of the great destinies of that people, whom, from the midst of camps, I first greeted with the name of great, etc." He mentioned neither liberal guarantees nor the Republic.

That word Republic worried him, obsessed him. He was going to rid himself of it, but little by little, timidly by successive omissions, as his victories gave him the strength and courage to do so.

In 1804, after the establishment of the Empire, not only the Fourteenth of July but the establishment of the republic were celebrated once again. In 1805 there was no longer any question of celebrating either of these events.

The newspaper stamp bore the legend

République française through December 31, 1805. The seal of the state was changed earlier; the law of 6 Pluviôse, Year XIII, removed all republican symbolism from it. In the formula for decrees Napoleon frequently called himself Emperor by the constitutions of the Republic until May 28, 1807. In the formula for the promulgation of laws, these words appeared for the last time in the law of April 29, 1806, in the code of civil procedure. Thereafter, it is "Napoleon by the Grace of God and the constitutions. . . ."

But the Emperor did not dare take formal and direct action against the use of the word Republic. It was only after the meeting at Erfurt (September–October 1808), when Alexander and he mutually guaranteed the submission of Europe, that he felt himself strong enough to abolish the last vestige of the Republic, by the decree of October 22, 1808, expressed in these words: "The coins which will be manufactured from January 1, 1809 onward will bear as legend, on the reverse side, the words: *Empire français,* in place of those of *République française.*" No one noticed this decree; the word Republic formerly considered by the people as a talisman of victory was forgotten, replaced in the imagination of the French people by the name of Napoleon, another talisman of victory. . . .

If we have defined the exact time when the word Republic disappeared, it is not out of vain curiosity. While that word survived, there was some tempering of despotism, and the despot believed himself obliged to observe a certain restraint, to appear reasonable. Once the word was erased, there remained almost no brake on the whims of his genius, and it is perhaps no exaggeration to say that then his tyranny became as insane as it was grandiose. . . .

The imperial despotism stopped the Revolution, marked a retrogression toward the principles of the *ancien régime,* provisionally abolished liberty, partially abolished equality. But it is the political results of the Revolution rather than the social results that were thus suppressed. Possession of national lands; civil laws codified into a code less egalitarian than that conceived by the Convention, but infinitely more humane, more reasonable than those of the *ancien régime,* having the advantage, moreover, of being uniform for all France; use of revolutionary laws on inheritance; all this code imposed on almost all Europe — that is how the social results of the Revolution survived. And it is this which explains that after his fall, when these results were challenged by the royalists returned from the emigration, Napoleon Bonaparte, who had repudiated the political work of the Revolution as much as he could, appeared to be and could call himself the man of the Revolution.

II. GUARDIAN OF FRONTIERS OR AGGRESSOR?

Emperor of the West

ADOLPHE THIERS

In this second selection from Adolphe Thiers' monumental *Histoire du Consulate et de l'Empire* the author presents his thesis that Napoleon had two foreign policies—one, before 1803, pacific and defensive, and the other, after 1803, belligerent and aggressive.

THE REPUBLICAN government of 1795, having ceased to be bloodthirsty without ceasing to be persecuting, had imposed peace on Spain, on Prussia, on North Germany, and remained engaged in a long drawn-out war with Austria, a stubborn war with England, war that it fought, so to speak, by habit, by means of admirable soldiers, of excellent but divided generals, when there suddenly appeared in the Army of the Alps a young artillery officer, short, of uncivilized but superb countenance, of strange but striking mind, in turn taciturn and prodigious of words, at one moment disgraced by the Republic and then relegated to the bureaus of the Directory, whose attention he attracted by his sound and profound opinions on each circumstance of the war, which won him the command of Paris on the day of 13 Vendémiaire and soon the command of the troops in Italy. Reappearing among them as commander-in-chief, he quickly imposed an extraordinary movement on events, crossed the Alps which, up until then, no one had ever been able to get through, invaded Lombardy, drew all the war there, vanquished the armies of Austria one after the other, wore down her persistence, wrung from her recognition of our conquests, forced her to agree to immense losses for herself, thus gave peace to the continent, and to his astonishing acts he added a language entirely new in its originality and its grandeur. That this extraordinary young man, appearing like a meteor on this troubled and bloody horizon, should not attract everyone's attention and not end by charming them was impossible! France would have been made of ice, which she never was, France would have had to succumb to him and the world with her. In fact she did succumb.

Among the powers to which the Revolution had thrown down the gauntlet, one alone remained to defeat; it was England. Withdrawn on her element, inaccessible to us as we were to her, it seemed that she could be neither defeated nor victorious. The Directory sought to occupy the conqueror of Italy, and regarding him not only as the greatest captain of the century but the most fruitful in resources, charged him with surmounting the physical obstacle that

From Adolphe Thiers, *Histoire du Consulate et de l'Empire* (Paris: Paulin, Lheureux et Cie., 1845–1862), XVII, 836–859. [Editor's translation.]

24

separates us from our eternal rival. The young Bonaparte, appointed general of the Army of the Ocean, finding the preparations that had been made to cross the Pas-de-Calais insufficient, wished to attack England in the East. He had the Egyptian Expedition mounted, with five hundred sails crossed the Mediterranean under the very eyes of Nelson, took Malta in passing, landed at the foot of the Column of Pompey, defeated the Mamelukes at the pyramids, the janissaries at Aboukir, and became master of Egypt and for several months indulged in marvelous dreams that embraced both the Orient and the Occident. Suddenly, on learning that the Directory by its anarchic nature had drawn war upon itself, and that thanks to its incapacity it conducted the war badly, General Bonaparte abandoned Egypt, crossed the sea a second time, and, by his sudden reappearance, surprised, delighted a harassed France. He had not been more prompt to desire power than France to offer it to him, because seeing him directing the war, administering conquered provinces, managing all things in a word, she had recognized in him a chief of empire as well as a great captain. Having become First Consul he signed within a space of two years the peace of the continent at Lunéville, the peace of the seas at Amiens, pacified the Vendée, reconciled the Church with the French Revolution, raised up altars, reestablished calm in France and in Europe, made the world, fatigued by a dozen years of bloody agitation, breathe again. Vested in 1802 with power for life in recompense for so many prodigies, he worked in an atmosphere of universal admiration to reestablish France and Europe! . . .

For the moment the young Consul had nothing to desire and left the world nothing to desire. His power was without limits, by virtue not only of laws but of universal support. He had that power for life, which was sufficient for a husband without children, and he had the power to choose his successor, which permitted him to regulate the future according to the public interest,

and according to his own affections. As for France, she had, thanks to the Revolution and to him, a position that she had never previously had in the world, and that she was not to have again, even when she would command from Cadiz to Lubeck. For frontiers she had the Alps, the Rhine, the Scheldt — that is to say, all that she could hope for her security and for her power, because beyond them were only acquisitions contrary to nature and contrary to good policy. She had crossed Italy to the Adige, taking care to give compensation in Germany to the Austrian princes who formerly held appanages there. Realizing that the principle of pontifical authority was highly necessary according to dogma, and highly useful according to politics, she had reestablished the Pope, who owed to her the security and the respect that he enjoyed and who expected from her the complete restoration of his states. She wisely disdained the impotent anger of the Bourbons of Naples. She regulated the situation of Switzerland with an admirable wisdom. Acknowledging at once large and small cantons, aristocratic cantons and democratic cantons, because there are all of these, forcing them to live in peace and in equality; putting an end to subjugation of classes, subjugations of territory; applying, in a word, the principles of 1789 in the Alps, without violating always invincible nature, she had given in the *acte de médiation* the model of all the future constitutions of Switzerland. It is in Germany especially that the profound wisdom of the consular policy manifested itself. There were the German princes despoiled of their states by the cession of the left bank of the Rhine to France; there were Austrian princes despoiled of their patrimony by the liberation of Italy. The First Consul had not thought that one could leave either the one or the other without compensation, and Germany without organization. The French Revolution had already posed in France the principle of secularization by confiscation of ecclesiastical property, and to use this principle to find compensations for the dispossessed princes was to extend it to Germany and to have it accepted by Germany. With what remained of the states of the archbishops of Trier, of Mainz, of Köln, with those of some other ecclesiastical princes, the First Consul had formed a mass of indemnities, sufficient to satisfy all the despoiled princely families and to maintain judicious equilibrium in Germany. After having cleverly combined the indemnities and the influences in the Confederation, and having assured suitable pensions for the dispossessed ecclesiastical princes, he had, after long and mature consideration, held back his plan, and not being presumptuous enough then to write treaties with his sword alone, he had associated Prussia with his work through self-interest, Russia through vanity, by these divers adhesions induced Austria to join him, and in obtaining the adoption of the recess of the Diet of 1803, accomplished a masterpiece of patient and profound policy. That recess, in fact, without engaging us too much in German affairs, brought order, calm, resignation to Germany and placed the balance of German interests in our hands. It especially prepared for us the sole alliance then desirable and possible, that of Prussia. France was at that moment so powerful, so feared, that with the alliance of a single state on the continent she was assured of the submission of the others, and with the continent subjugated, England would have to swallow in silence her chagrin at seeing her rival so great. But that alliance could then be found in Prussia and only in Prussia. Austria having lost the Low Countries, Swabia, almost all of Italy, and the ecclesiastical principalities that formed her clientele in Germany, was the great victim of the French Revolution in Europe, and that was an inevitable difficulty. Policy recommended treating her with respect, even paying her damages if it were possible, but did not permit hoping to find in her a friend, an ally. Russia could give an alliance only at the cost of disastrous concessions in the East. With her, courtesy without intimacy and almost without contact was necessary. There remained Prussia, with which, in fact, it was easy to have an understanding. That power, gorged with the property of the church and asking nothing better than to have more of it, had become that which in France was called an *acquéreur des biens nationaux*. In respecting her, in favoring her, without nevertheless pushing Austria to the limit, one was certain to have her on our side. Her prudent and good monarch was charmed by the policy of the First Consul and sought his friendship. The alliance with Prussia assured us from that moment the submission of the continent and the resignation of proud England. The First Consul had obtained from the latter, by the Peace of Amiens, the recognition of our conquests, and, the most difficult situation to make her accept, the conquest of Antwerp. With her there was only one more difficulty to overcome; it was to get ourselves pardoned, by dint of circumspection, for so many grandeurs acquired in a few years. And it could be done, because the English admired the First Consul with all the vivacity of British infatuation, at least equal to Parisian infatuation. An act of flattery from him, in descending from the height of his genius as from the highest of thrones, was certain to touch English pride deeply. It was possible that flattery would not always be returned for flattery; but, having reached by then the pinnacle of glory, if some English orators, or some émigré journalists were to try to insult him, he could ignore it, and leave to the world, to the English nation itself, the task of avenging him.

One power remained, formerly very considerable, much in decline at this time: Spain, still under the sceptre of the Bourbons, but fallen into such a state of decomposition, and in that state so prostrate at the feet of the First Consul, that to govern it from Paris he had only to speak a word to the poor Charles IV or to the miserable Godoy. As this decomposition was allowed to reach its ultimate stage, this power [Spain] could soon be seen begging from the First Consul not only a policy, which she had already done, but a government, a king perhaps!

What was left to be desired, for him, for France, the happy mortal who had become the chief? Nothing, only to be faithful to his policy, which was that of force tempered by moderation. The conqueror of Rivoli, of the pyramids, of Marengo, author also of the Concordat, of the treaties of Lunéville and Amiens, of the Swiss *acte de médiation,* of the recess of the Diet of 1803, of the Civil Code, of the recall of the émigrés, had more divers glories than any mortal before him had ever had. If one merit could be lacking from the sum of all his merits, it was perhaps in not having given liberty to France. But then the fear of liberty, far from being a pretext of servility, was an insurmountable sentiment. For the generation of 1800, liberty was the scaffold, the schism, the war in the Vendée, bankruptcy, confiscation. The only liberty that France needed then was the moderation of a great man. But, alas, the moderation of a great man, endowed with all powers, endowed also with all talents, is it not among all the revolutionary chimeras the most chimeric?

Liberty, even when it is out of fashion, is nevertheless missed all the more strongly where it no longer exists. This man, so admirable then for the very reason that he could dare anything, was on the edge of an abyss. In fact the Peace of Amiens was scarcely signed, and the joy of the peace had scarcely cooled among the English, yet the grandeur of France still remained for them to see, dazzling like a troublesome light, unfortunately too little dissimulated in the person of the First Consul. Some caresses for Mr. Fox, on a visit to Paris, did not prevent the First Consul from having the attitude of the master not only of the affairs of France but of the affairs of Europe. His language, full of genius and ambition, offended the pride of the English, his ravenous activity troubled their peace of mind. He sent an army to San Domingo, which was certainly permissible, but he publicly sent Colonel Sébastiani to Turkey,

Colonel Savary to Egypt, General Decaen to India, charged with missions of observation which could scarcely be mistaken for scientific missions. It was more than was necessary to awaken British suspicion. At that time some émigrés, obstinately remaining in England despite the glory and the clemency of the First Consul, published writings against him and his family that the universal disapproval of England would have smothered a year earlier, but that to-day, its imprudently excited jealousy complacently welcomed and its laws did not permit it to forbid. It was indeed the case for disdain, because what summit was more lofty than that on which was placed the First Consul to regard from on high the indignities of calumny? Alas, he descended from that glorious pinnacle to listen to the pamphleteers, and to give himself over to fits of outrage as violent as they were unworthy of him. To insult him, the wise, the victorious, what unforgivable crime! As if at all times, in all countries, free or not, genius, virtue, charity were not insulted! No, torrents of blood must flow because pamphleteers abusing their government every day, had insulted a foreigner, great man without doubt, but man after all, and moreover chief of a rival nation!

From that instant the challenge was thrown between the warrior in whom was summed up the French Revolution, and the English people, whose jealousy had been too little humored. Within a few days Malta would have been evacuated, and, by a strange fatality, it happened that at that moment when all the Britannic passions were excited, the First Consul, exercising in Switzerland his benevolent dictatorship, sent an army to Berne. A weak ministry, humble servant of Britannic passions, sought here a pretext to suspend the evacuation of Malta. If the First Consul had been patient, if he had insisted firmly but gently, the frivolity of the British motive would not have permitted long deferment of the solemnly promised evacuation of the great Mediterranean fortress. But the First Consul, feeling more than the sentiment of offended pride, that of wounded justice, asked that the treaties be executed, because there was, he said, no power that could with impunity break its word to France and to him. Everyone recalls the sadly heroic scene with Lord Whitworth, and the rupture of the Peace of Amiens. The First Consul swore then to perish or to punish England. Disastrous oath! The émigrés, we refer to the irreconcilables, did not limit themselves to writing, they conspired. The First Consul with his penetrating eye discovered plots that the police knew not how to discover, struck at the conspirators, and believing to perceive among them some princes, not being able to seize those who appeared to be the truly guilty, went into Germany, without concern for international law, to arrest the descendant of the Condés. He had him shot without mercy, and himself, the severe critic of January 21, equalled regicide as closely as he could and seemed to experience a kind of satisfaction in committing it in the face of Europe, in contempt of it. The wise Consul had suddenly become a madman with two frenzies: the frenzy of a wounded man who breathes only vengeance, the frenzy of a victor gladly defying the enemies he is sure to conquer. Then the better to defy his adversaries and to satisfy at once his ambition and his anger, he placed the imperial crown on his head. Europe, offended and intimidated at the same time took a new view of France and her leader. At the sound of the fusillade at Vincennes, Prussia, who was going to conclude a formal alliance, drew back, kept her silence, and renounced a friendship that ceased to be honorable. Austria, more calculating, made no overt reaction, but profited from the occasion to overstep the line in the execution of the recess of 1803. The young Emperor of Russia, good and full of honor, alone dared to ask, as guarantor of the Germanic constitution, for an explanation of the violation of the territory of Baden. Napoleon replied to him with an insulting allusion to the death of Paul I. The Tsar said nothing but was deeply offended. Prussia chilled, Austria encouraged in her excesses, Russia outraged — in these frames of mind they were witnesses to the beginning of our struggle with England.

Then the Boulogne expedition was prepared. Napoleon would have been able slowly to organize his navy and direct distant expeditions against the English colonies, leaving the continent, ill-disposed but intimidated, in peace, to wait until his expeditions caused noticeable injury to England, until our privateers devastated her commerce, and until she grew tired of a war in which we could do little against her, but in which she could do nothing against us, our trade being then purely continental. But that powerful genius, the greatest victor over physical difficulties who had perhaps ever existed, wanted to struggle with England hand to hand and was justified, because if it was permitted to anyone to attempt the passage of the Straits of Calais with a numerous army, it was to him without any doubt. . . . That man who had the greatest of difficulties to overcome, that of crossing the sea with an army of 150,000 soldiers, who needed consequently the perfect immobility of the continent — that audacious man, having gone to assume the crown of Italy at Milan, declared on his own authority that Genoa would be joined to the Empire. Immediately the European coalition was formed anew. Russia, deeply wounded by the insult that she had received from the First Consul, but offended also by the maritime pretention of England, had thought to serve as mediator, and had continued to press for the evacuation of Malta. On receiving the news of the annexation of Genoa, she asked nothing more; she formed a coalition with England and Austria, set her arms in motion, and promised to bring along Prussia in passing, Prussia still held in check by the prudence and moderation of her king. Thus from that day the wise pacifier of 1803 had become the provoker of a general war, solely by having failed to master his passions!

But this man was a man of genius, like Alexander or Caesar, and fortune pardons much and long to genius. The threats from the continent had not interrupted the preparations for his great expedition; the mistake of an admiral caused it to fail, and that was fortunate, because if he had been embarked at the moment when the Austrian army crossed the Inn, it would have been possible that, while he opened the route to London, the Austrian army would open that to Paris. However that may be, his expedition postponed, he threw himself like a lion who leaps from one enemy onto another, moved quickly in a few days from Boulogne to Ulm, from Ulm to Austerlitz, crushed Austria and Russia, then saw Prussia, which had gone to join Europe, fall trembling at his feet and ask pardon of the conqueror of the coalition!

From that moment the war with England was converted into a continental war, and that was certainly not a misfortune if one knew how to behave politically as well as militarily. The powers of the continent, in taking up arms for England, furnished us with a battlefield that we lacked, a battlefield where we found Ulm and Austerlitz in place of Trafalgar. There was nothing to complain about. But after having soundly defeated and convinced them of the inanity of their efforts, it was necessary to behave toward them in such a manner that they would not be tempted to begin again; it was necessary to punish Austria without pushing her to despair, even to console her for her great misfortunes, if an indemnification could be obtained for her; it was necessary to leave Russia in her confusion, in the impotence resulting from distance; and as for Prussia, finally, it was necessary not to abuse her too much for her mistakes, nor scoff at her too much for her miscarried mediation; it was necessary to demonstrate to her the danger of giving in to the passions of factions, to attach her definitively by giving her some of the rich spoils of victory, and then return with our victorious forces toward England, henceforth deprived of allies, frightened by her isolation, assailed by our privateers, threatened by a formidable expedition. Reason

declared and the facts proved that she would not have waited for others to negotiate with her defeated allies; indeed, she negotiated herself. They would have had the Peace of Amiens expanded.

After Ulm and Austerlitz Napoleon found himself in a unique position to realize in Europe that wise and profound policy, which would have consisted of separating the continent from England, and thus forcing the latter to make peace. Austria, accustomed to struggling for five years, three years at least, against us, in two months saw herself invaded as far as Vienna and Brunn, losing entire armies in a day, reduced to laying down arms as did Mack, and no longer had any idea of resisting us, at least as long as she was not pushed to the last degree of despair. The young Emperor of Russia, who, at the head of the soldiers of Suvorov, had believed himself capable of playing an important role and had played only a very humiliating one, had fallen into an extreme state of dejection. Prussia, who, with 200,000 soldiers of the great Frederick, had come to Vienna to lay down the law and found us in a position to dictate to everyone, was at once trembling and almost ridiculous. How easy, fitting, adroit it would have been to be generous toward such enemies!

Without doubt one could not make a friend of Austria, and we have said why; but in deciding at that time not to make her an ally of France it was not necessary to add needlessly to her grievances and to change them into implacable hate. In compensation for the Low Countries, Swabia, Milanais, and the clientage of the ecclesiastical states that she had lost, she had been given the Venetian States. To take them back from her was harsh. Nevertheless, as war cannot be a game that costs nothing to those who stir it up, it is understandable that the Venetian States were taken back, although the motive of liberating Italy could not be decently claimed, since we had taken Piedmont and converted Lombardy into an apanage of the Bonaparte family. But in depriving Austria of Venice, depriving her also of Trieste, depriving her of Illyria, as Napoleon then did, to take from her all outlet to the sea, to reduce her to suffocate within her continental territory, was a severity without real profit for us and which could only drive her to despair. Not even to stop there, to rob her also of the Tyrol, the Vorarlberg, the remainder of Swabia to enrich Bavaria, Würtemberg, and Baden, small and treacherous allies who were to exploit us in order the better to betray us, this was to make her implacable. To treat people thus it is necessary to kill them, and if they cannot be killed, it is to make enemies for oneself, who, on the first occasion, stab one in the back, and who have the right to do it.

To deprive Austria of the Venetian States, sole consolation for all her losses, was harsh, we say, and nevertheless resulted almost inevitably from the Third Coalition. The good policy would have consisted in finding for her a compensation for that inevitable severity. . . .

Far from thinking of indemnifying her, Napoleon thought only to despoil her, to scoff at her, to make her a victim of the times even more than the times demanded. He took from her now without compensation, and independently of the Venetian States, Illyria, Tyrol, Vorarlberg, the remainder of Swabia. In general one punished in order to remove the desire to begin again; here, far from removing the desire, this kindled the passion for it in the heart of Austria. As for Prussia Napoleon had only one thought, that of ridiculing her. Certainly he had plenty of pretext for it. M. d'Haugewitz, arriving in Vienna in the name of his king, whom the Tsar had led to war through the intermediary of a thoughtless nobility and a beautiful and imprudent queen, M. d'Haugewitz, arriving on the eve of Austerlitz to dictate the law, and the next day receiving it on his knees, presented a comic spectacle, as the world sometimes offers them. But if it is permissible to laugh at human affairs, often laughable certainly, it is when one observes them, it is never when one directs them.

Napoleon had all the caprices of power at once; he wanted to do what pleased him and wanted to be able to laugh besides. That was too much, a hundred times too much!

In asking him for Hanover for her archdukes, Austria gave him the idea, which he found clever, to make the allies of England accept the spoils of England. Only, in place of giving Hanover to Austria, he presented it to Prussia. . . . Napoleon offered Hanover to Prussia with the sword at her throat. "Hanover or war," he seemed to say to M. d'Haugewitz, who did not hesitate, and who preferred Hanover. Napoleon was not content there, and he made her pay for that already bitter gift by the sacrifice of the Marquisate of Anspach and of the Duchy of Berg, so that he diminished the gift without diminishing the shame. It was, moreover, an act of grave imprudence, because it made war with England interminable. In fact, it was impossible that the old George III would ever consent to give up the patrimony of his family, and the English kings then had in the republican monarchy of England an influence that they no longer have. M. d'Haugewitz, who left Potsdam for Schönbrunn to the great applause of the court, who left to lay down the law to France, and to declare war on her for the benefit of England, now returned to Berlin after having received the law, and bringing back the most beautiful of Britannic spoils. How greatly disturbed must have been a good king, a proud nation, a vain and impassioned court!

Thus Napoleon, instead of drawing from his incomparable victory of Austerlitz continental peace and maritime peace, a double peace that he could have easily secured by frightening or buying off England's allies forever, had mortified some, humiliated others, and left to all a war of desperation as sole resource. He had even created an invincible obstacle to peace by the gift of Hanover to Prussia.

Everything was faulty in the arrangements of Vienna in 1806, but Napoleon did not confine himself to these mistakes, already so grave. When he returned to Paris, an intoxication of ambition, unknown in modern times, usurped his mind. Henceforth he thought of an immense empire, supported by vassal kingdoms, which would dominate Europe and would be designated by a name consecrated by the Romans and by Charlemagne, Empire of the West. Napoleon had already prepared two vassal kingdoms, in the Cisalpine Republic converted into the Kingdom of Italy, and in the state of Naples taken from the Bourbons to give to his brother Joseph. He added Holland, converted from republic into monarchy and given to Louis Bonaparte. But that was not all. The Empire of the West to be complete should embrace Germany. Napoleon had created there as allies the princes of Bavaria, of Würtemberg, of Baden. To them he abandoned the spoils of Austria, of Prussia, of the unsecularized ecclesiastical princes, abandoned to them what nobility was left, made them kings, and asked of them princesses, whom they delivered with alacrity, for his brothers, his adopted children, and his lieutenants. At that moment Germany, which had not yet recovered from the upheavals that the system of secularizations had produced, about which a mass of questions remained to be solved, fell into a state of extraordinary disorder. The sovereign princes, whether electors or kings, pillaged the property of the nobility and of the Church, failed to pay the pensions of the dispossessed ecclesiastical princes, and all the oppressed appealed, not to vanquished Austria nor Prussia, struck by ridicule, but to the sole master of existence, that is, Napoleon. From that universal recourse, to him was born the idea of a new Germanic Confederation, which would bear the title of Confederation of the Rhine, and would be placed under the protection of Napoleon. It was composed of Bavaria, Würtemberg, Baden, Nassau, and all the princes of the south of Germany. Thus the Emperor of the West, mediator of Switzerland, protector of the Confederation of the Rhine, suzerain of the kingdoms of Naples, Italy,

Holland, had only Spain to add to these vassal states, and he would then be more powerful than Charlemagne. That high in Napoleon's vast brain had risen the fumes of pride.

In the presence of such a dislocation, Francis II, not being able to retain the title of Emperor of Germany, abdicated that title to call himself henceforth only Emperor of Austria. It was, after all his losses of territory, the most humiliating of degradations. Prussia, she too chased out of the old Germanic Confederation, took the expedient of gathering around her the princes of north Germany, and of thus making herself the chief of a little Germany reduced by one-third. She asked permission for it, which was coldly granted, with the secret thought of discouraging those who would be tempted to confederate with her. ... In fact in the course of the Middle Ages Germany, not being able to achieve unity, had remained a federated state. While reserving their independence, the states that composed it had federated themselves in order to defend themselves against their powerful neighbors, and naturally against the most powerful of all, against France. To that France had responded by a wholly natural and wholly legitimate policy. Profiting from German jealousies, she had supported the petty princes against the great, and Prussia against Austria. But to go from that traditional and legitimate policy to create a Germanic Confederation that would not be German but French, which would burden us with all the affairs of the Germans, would expose us to all their hates, would give us erstwhile allies destined to be traitors of the morrow, was the madness of ambition and nothing more. In all countries that have a traditional policy, there exists an objective assigned by that policy and towards which one advances more or less quickly according to the times. To make in each epoch one step toward that objective, is to progress naturally. To make more than one is imprudent; to want to make them all at once is to condemn oneself certainly to miss the objective in bypassing it. By the recess of 1803, Napoleon had approached as closely as possible to the objective of our traditional policy in Germany. By the Confederation of the Rhine he had disastrously passed it. He was thus in international law what the Jacobins had been in social law. They had wanted to remake society, he wanted to remake Europe. They had employed the guillotine, he employed cannon. The means were infinitely less odious and surrounded, moreover, with the prestige of glory. They were scarcely more sensible.

Revolutionary Expansionist

ALBERT SOREL

Albert Sorel (1842–1906), trained in the law, began his career as a diplomat in the French foreign ministry but soon gave it up to devote himself to teaching—in the École libre des Sciences politiques—and to writing. His major work was L'Europe et la Révolution française. The first of its eight volumes, on the spirit and methods of European diplomacy of the ancien régime, was published in 1885; three volumes on the diplomatic history of the Revolution to 1795 appeared eight years later, and in 1903 and 1904 came the four final volumes, largely on the foreign policy of Napoleon. He emphasized, first, the continuity of French foreign policy from the ancien régime through the Revolution to Napoleon, who carried on the policy of his predecessors; and second, the unwavering determination of Britain to deny France her "natural frontiers," a judgment that perhaps reflected the anti-British feeling common in France after Fashoda and during the Boer War. Sorel developed his interpretation most fully in Volume VI, from which this selection is taken.

HUMAN AFFAIRS can be grasped only at their origins, in their first emergence from the soul. As they move away from the sources, the waters become mixed, the slope carries them away, and the river is henceforth only a formidable weight that falls; one follows their direction, but the waters have lost their transparency. The first hours of the Consulate, its acts and words, are filled with destiny; it is necessary to stop there in order to understand the sequel of that story, to grasp its connections and to determine the central threads that will enable us to find our way in the immense unfolding that is beginning.

Everything happens at the same time, everything proceeds at the same pace, the organization of France and its extension in Europe. But while within, the Revolution, subdued, casts itself more and more in the old mold, outside it breaks the old forms and overflows; it is there that its imprint remains the strongest and that its impulse will continue to carry France for the longest time. Bonaparte admired the Committee of Public Safety for having revived the policy of Richelieu and that of Louis XIV. The Directory had only continued that

From Albert Sorel, L'Europe et la Révolution française (Paris: Plon-Nourrit et Cie., 17th edition, 1922), VI, 18–23, 31, 34–36. Reprinted by permission of Librairie Plon. All rights reserved by Librairie Plon. [Editor's translation.]

policy, in exaggerating it and disfiguring it; Bonaparte follows it, by deliberate design, in adding to it method, the correlation of parties, the continuous and concerted progress of the whole. He had dossiers prepared of the major affairs in progress, those that the Committee had undertaken, those whose direction the Directory had already reserved for itself: the affairs of Prussia and those of Spain in particular. It is necessary always to have these affairs in mind.

The provisional executive council, in 1792, had designated the Rhine as the frontier of the Republic; the Committee of Public Safety of the Year III had negotiated the cession of that frontier to France. In order to obtain it, to indemnify the German princes dispossessed on the left bank, the Committee had proposed the secularization of the ecclesiastical principalities of the right bank, that is, the territorial consolidation of Germany for the benefit of the lay princes associated with the Republic. It had foreseen the necessity of combining the continent against England in order to force her to recognize France's possession of the frontiers of Gaul and, to achieve it, the committee had offered to Spain the conquest of Portugal, to Prussia supremacy in northern Germany, to Austria compensations in Bavaria and in Italy. The Directory had continued that work at the Congress of Rastadt, won over the German princes to secularization, negotiated indemnities with Prussia; offered to Frederick-William, for his alliance, the imperial crown and the annexation of Hanover; allied with Spain, forced Portugal to submit; bordered France with client and tributary republics – the Batavian, the Helvetic, the Cisalpine; occupied Piedmont, dismembered the Papal States, republicanized Rome and Naples, subjugated Tuscany and tried to form of all these governments an enormous body for the investment and blockade of England. The Mediterranean under the domination of France, *the Mediterranean, French lake,* formed the complement of that magnificent design of republican expansion.

Bonaparte is nourished on this. It is by having, at one moment, decided its success, by the campaign in Italy and by the Treaty of Campo Formio, that he became the most popular of the generals and the first personnage of the Republic; it is to consummate the work, so compromised, that he returned from Egypt, in 1799, and that he made himself Consul. France expects of him the accomplishment of the design that is for her the condition and the guarantee of peace, the termination of the Revolution, the triumph and the splendor of the Republic. That is the price of his reign. It is the master thought, the permanent object of his policy; his superiority is to know the means to achieve that end, to pursue them constantly and to know how to concert them.

But it did not suffice that the victories of Masséna, of Lecourbe, of Moreau, of Brune had delivered the Republic; they simply restored it to the situation of 1795. It is necessary to restore it to the situation of 1798, at the moment when Europe renewed the war, and to establish it there definitively. As for abandoning a single one of the conquests of France, he does not think of it, he never thought of it. The motives that caused these countries to be invaded, in order to conquer the frontiers, require their occupation to maintain these frontiers. They are the European hostages of the Republic, it is by them that the Republic will force Europe first to sign the peace and then to respect it. It is in Holland that England has been repulsed; it is in Italy that Austria has been coerced and will be again: Holland must be held, if one wishes to hold Belgium; it is necessary to have Piedmont, if one wishes to assure communications with the Cisalpine Republic; Genoa, Milan, Rome, Naples must be allied, if not subjugated, in order to drive back the Austrians in the north of Italy and to correct that weakness of Campo-Formio: Venice and a part of the mainland given to Austria. Moreover, the domination of Italy is the condition of that supremacy of the Mediterranean which the

Egyptian Expedition made the favorite conception of Bonaparte.

"It is not to return shamefully within our former frontiers," that we have fought this desperate war, said, in the Year III, Merlin de Douai in the name of the Committee of Public Safety. It is not to retreat before Austria and to deliver Italy to her, to restore the petty king of Piedmont and to deliver to him the keys of Provence; it is not to give way before the English, on land and on sea, to abandon to them Holland, Belgium, the Mediterranean that the republican armies conquered in 1799. France would not pardon it. It would see in it a betrayal of the liberated peoples, the sacrifice of France's proudest accomplishment: the enthusiastic crusade of 1792 and the magnificence of the Italian expeditions.

France believes that these peoples are free only because she admits them to the honors of the Republic, gives them her laws and receives them into her heavenly city. The judgment of Bonaparte on that matter is only the popular prejudice rationalized by a statesman. He regards these peoples with the superior attitude of an "enlightened" Frenchman of the eighteenth century who takes his jurisprudence with the reign of law. His code of the law of nations, that will be the decree of December 15, 1792, coordinated by a lawyer of *Chambres de réunion*. And that work of state, which was in the eyes of members of the Convention, a work of justice, remains in his eyes a work of high and just policy. The Frenchman, champion of the rights of humanity, interpreter of universal reason, is called, by his Revolution, to govern the universe. The universe must not refuse it; he who resists is a rebel. To be admitted into the Republic appeared to members of the Convention the highest reward of a liberated people, which it should earn by a long stage of preparation and by considerable tributes; to be admitted into the Empire will soon appear to Napoleon, as it appeared to the Romans, the good fortune of elected and initiated people.

Now the Republic cannot and should not

retreat. That is the spirit of the proclamation that Bonaparte addressed to the armies on December 25, 1799, at the same time that he announced the program of the Consulate. Above all, to assure to France "the heritage of the Gauls," and in order to assure it, to carry the war beyond it:

You are the same men who conquered Holland, the Rhine and Italy and made peace under the walls of an astonished Vienna. Soldiers! it is no longer your frontiers that must be defended; enemy states must be invaded.

"All is defense," he said to Bernadotte, in the Council of State, "all is defense, even conquest that becomes the necessary consequence of the war." And everything, by these immense convolutions, these random ricochets, aims at England. He said to Roederer in December 1800,

England cannot want peace, because we are masters of the world. Spain is ours. We have a foot in Italy. In Egypt we hold the rears of their positions. Switzerland, Holland, Belgium. . . . There is one condition irrevocably determined and for which we declared to Prussia, to Russia, to the Emperor that we would, if necessary, make war alone against all, that condition is that there be no stadtholder in Holland and that we shall keep Belgium and the left bank of the Rhine.

It is necessary now to make the sea useless and deadly for the English, blockade them in their island, wear them down, ruin them, invade them, enchain them; to turn to their confusion, to their subjugation, to their isolation from the world, that insular location that is the source of their insolence, their wealth, and their supremacy. "In the present situation of Europe," he wrote to Spanish Admiral Mazarredo, blockaded in Brest, "I attach the greatest importance to the break-out of two squadrons; would they only drive off the English squadron for twenty-four hours and then return." That is to say, to prove that one can hold the sea, force the passage, gain the time that Caesar and William of Normandy lacked. And to Lucien:

We do not flatter ourselves to have peace while Pitt remains in the ministry. That man will not abandon an atom of the empire of the seas, short of being forced to it by war, and while I can wield a sword I shall never recognize that unjust domination of our rivals. . . . We must have new continental victories. It is by controlling all the coast of Europe that we can bring Pitt to an honorable peace. . . . If the seas escape us, there is no harbor, no river mouth, no river that would not be within the reach of our sword. . . .

If Bonaparte continued against Europe the invasions of Louis XIV and of the Convention, Europe continued against Bonaparte the War of the Spanish Succession and the coalitions of 1792 to 1798. Neither in London, nor in Vienna, nor in Berlin did the event of Brumaire appear to have the importance that history later attributed to it. The usurpation of the Republic by a general of the army was foreseen from the beginning of the Revolution. Bonaparte did not yet possess the prestige that his Consulate gave him. The politicians did not see in him the statesman, and the military men appreciated in the conqueror of Italy only a juggler of victories, an adventurer, lucky especially to have encountered only the exhausted Austrians and not to have had to measure himself against either the army of Frederick or that of Suvorov. Agents in Paris persisted in depicting France in anarchy, ready to throw herself at the feet of the "King," to resume her former boundaries, in order to obtain peace. They presented the new government as a band of filibusters, mixed with charlatans, who would very quickly fall, like their predecessors, into public contempt. They spread ridiculous and scandalous anecdotes about the Consul, his household, his tribe of starving Corsicans. Corruption, treason especially, as in the time of the Directory — everything remained precarious, at the mercy of a plot or of a defeat.

It is then that the letter of Bonaparte to

King George, dated December 25, arrived in London. Pitt finds it "very polite in form," but, he writes to a friend, "the present situation of France does not yet offer us solid enough ground to promise any security in negotiations. . . . I believe that that can be expressed in a way to make clear to the French people that the shortest route to peace would be to effect the restoration of the monarchy, and, by that, to increase the chances of that result, the most desirable that the war can have." Such was the spirit of the reply that Grenville addressed to Talleyrand on January 4, 1800. These were England's permanent peace conditions; she had posed them in 1793; she made them prevail only in 1814, and they were such that neither the French nation nor the First Consul could think for an instant of accepting them: the withdrawal to the old frontiers, with the monarchy as a guarantee. That was the ruin of the Revolution, the renunciation of conquests, the abandonment of the plan of European supremacy, things that the French of that time confused, as did the English themselves, with the Republic.

The English dream of major war — after little expeditions "to pillage, to trouble, to distract troops" — "to risk, if our forces will permit it, a large army, either in Brittany, with the idea of taking Brest with the aid of the royalists; or, between the Seine and the Somme, with the intention of occupying at least the land between the two rivers and of striking terror in the capital, even without advancing there." At that point arrives a message from Talleyrand, declaring anew the pacific intentions of France. Grenville replies to it on January 20 with a refusal to continue the correspondence. The next day Parliament meets. Pitt announces his war policy to the Commons; he paints, in violent and excessive colors, France as a disorganized society, without finances, torn by factions, become the prey of military dictatorship and having only one desire: the return of its kings. He concluded with a quotation from the *Philippiques* of Cicero: "I am too sincere a friend of peace to sacrifice it, and to seize upon the shadow of it when reality is not truly within my reach. *Cur igitur pacem nolo? Qui infida est, quia periculosa, quia esse non potest."* Grenville went farther, if possible, in the House of Lords: "We must sustain the war energetically against a power that wishes to subjugate the world in order to ravage it."

Pitt returned to the charge on February 12: "Was it ever proved that the Jacobinism of Robespierre, of Barras, of the five directors, of the triumvirate disappeared because it resides completely in a single man, raised and nourished within its bosom, who is at once the son and the champion of all these atrocities?"

Peacemaker

ARTHUR LÉVY

Arthur Lévy (1847–1931) first attracted attention in the debate over Napoleon by the publication of his book, *Napoléon intime*, in 1893. In it the author sought to refute and counteract the portrait, drawn by the Emperor's detractors, of a ruthless, inhuman Napoleon; Lévy went to the opposite extreme, depicting him as a kind and amiable individual. A decade later he joined in the controversy over Napoleon's motives and aims in foreign affairs with the publication of a substantial volume, *Napoléon et la paix*. In it he explored in detail the relations of France with Prussia in 1806 and 1807 and incidentally to that subject had a great deal to say on Napoleon's relations with both Prussia and England in earlier years. His purpose throughout was to demonstrate the validity of his contention that Napoleon always sought peace and had war forced upon him. The selection is taken from the second book.

BEFORE his conquests, as after, Napoleon always had a profound desire to see peace reestablished in Europe. In that purpose he passionately sought the Prussian alliance, and far from wishing to make war on Prussia, as he was one day forced to do by a challenge of Frederick William III, farther still from wishing to destroy that kingdom he had, during long years, no other design than to strengthen it and to add to its territory. His intentions in that regard were manifested as soon as, so to speak, he played a political role. Scarcely returned from his first Italian campaign, he said to Sandoz-Rollin, who resided in Paris as chargé d'affaires of the Cabinet of Berlin: "France ought to favor Prussia in the compensations that will be granted to her at the Congress of Rastatt; Prussia is her friendly and natural ally."

Napoleon, returned from Egypt, found nothing changed in the foreign policy of France *vis-à-vis* Prussia. He hastened to resume his place among the zealous partisans of the Prussian alliance. About two weeks before the 18th of Brumaire he praised the qualities of Frederick William III to Sandoz-Rollin:

From Arthur Lévy, *Napoléon et la paix* (Paris: Plon-Nourrit & Cie., 1902), pp. 1–2, 12–14, 19–22, 24–25, 60–63, 65–69. Reprinted by permission of Librairie Plon. All rights reserved by Librairie Plon. [Editor's translation.]

Nothing attests better to the truth of the great praises that are lavished on the King of Prussia than his political conduct in this war. He retains his power while others lose it; he knows how to make his people happy and he will be the one to whom they will rally, in case of need, for the return of order and peace.

Some days later, Bonaparte did not hesitate, before the same listener, to treat Frederick William III as worthy successor of Frederick the Great, a compliment whose exaggeration made its sincerity suspect, for could he think seriously of putting in parallel the incomparable chief of state, iron-handed organizer, audacious captain, resolute statesman who was Frederick the Great and the lymphatic, complaisant, timid prince who at present reigned in Prussia?

But having given himself the task of succeeding whatever the circumstances, Napoleon, wishing to do more and better than his predecessors, did not disdain the classic procedures: public homage, indirect flattery, by which the favor of sovereigns is obtained. And one of his very first acts, as soon as he had the government in hand, was the dispatch of the following letter to Frederick William III.

Great and dear friend, one of our first démarches in taking the reins of the French government is to inform Your Majesty of our intention to execute existing treaties religiously.

We do not doubt that you on your side will do that which rests with you to tighten the bonds that unite the two states. We have as a guarantee of it the loyal character that distinguishes the actions of Your Majesty.

He has before him a great career and a long reign to traverse. He will find, in all circumstances and especially in the matter of the general peace, in the Consuls of the Republic, sentiments of friendship, as much more effective if Your Majesty, from his side, will continue freely to declare himself the friend of our Republic.

We express sincere wishes for the prosperity and glory of Your Majesty.

> — The Consuls of the Republic:
> Bonaparte, Sieyès, Roger-Ducos.

That declaration was not merely the act of simple courtesy by which a foreign power is informed of a change of government; it sought to obtain that which had been so often sought: a free and public promise of friendship for the French Republic. That promise, in the mind of the Consuls and particularly of Bonaparte, was to have as result the assurance of the peace of Europe. To achieve that goal, nothing is spared; first is proclaimed the respect of treaties, then is evoked the great career that opens before the King. "The treaties," that means the secret articles of the Treaty of Basel, by which France assured Prussia, when a general peace should be concluded, an important expansion in compensation for the Rhine provinces that she gave up. "The great career," is it not a new allusion to the offer of the imperial crown already formulated in 1796 by the Directory? Such was indeed the thought of the consular government, which will be explicitly repeated, at the end of 1803, in these terms:

By a secret article in the treaty of alliance, the two parties should henceforth use their influence to direct the minds of the Electors so that upon the vacancy of the imperial throne, which the invalid state of the Emperor Francis could make imminent, that crown would be placed on the head of the king of Prussia.

Desirous of showing that the letter of the Consuls indeed expressed his own sentiments and that he was personally a partisan of the Franco-Prussian alliance — affirming already his preponderance over his colleagues — Napoleon charged his first aide-de-camp, Colonel Duroc, to carry the consular missive and to deliver it into the hands of the King. . . .

He [Duroc] returned to Paris, intoxicated by the marks of cordiality that he had received, satisfied with the royal family, with the ministers, with everybody. He was the bearer of the reply of the King to the letter of the Consuls. That reply contained only the banal greetings and the unctuous compliments that are the framework of royal letters of this type: "My wishes for the happiness of France have been demonstrated on every occasion that has offered itself."

Bonaparte did not hide that the letter of the King was a check for the personal policy that he wished to inaugurate. He had in the end obtained nothing more than fine assurances, always platonic, always the same, that Prussia had not tired of giving for the past five years. He did not slacken his efforts to transform a neutrality that one could believe to be sympathetic into real friendship. He thought, like his predecessors, that with the aid of the Prussian alliance, England would be easily induced to make peace, because that alliance would permit France: (1) to counterbalance the power of Austria, openly in the pay of England; (2) to have the possibility of occupying, or to have occupied, Hanover, the only vulnerable point of England on the continent; (3) to close the northern ports to the English flag. . . .

None of these ideas is the invention of Bonaparte. In the Committee of Public Safety, in the Convention, from the deputy Dersaint to Brissot, Danton, Barère, and others, and the members of the Directory, all energetically demanded the invasion of England, the seizure of Hanover, already indicated under Louis XV by M. d'Argenson; all also had proclaimed the continental blockade as the supreme means of forcing England to restore peace to Europe. To force England to stop the trading in subsidies that she had exercised for eight years, making contracts, so much per man, so much per horse, to arm Europe against France; to induce the Cabinet of London to sign an honorable peace; to see only the goal, to relax not a minute his efforts to attain it, to scorn the obstacles on the road that he had not chosen and that he believed himself forced to follow, that was the obsession of Napoleon, perhaps his madness; but was it not a noble madness to refuse to allow France to fall to the rank of a secondary power, to refuse to recognize the right to abandon the frontiers watered with the blood of thousands of children of

France? By fidelity to that program, become for him unalterable and sacred, Napoleon would have his eyes fixed on Prussia for long years, and if he could not find in her an effective ally, he wanted always to doubt her hostility, more or less skillfully dissimulated but real nevertheless; he begged the Cabinet of Berlin to take the initiative of a mediation with the courts of the north in favor of peace.

Austria, having reconstituted her forces during the winter of 1799, prepared to take up arms again. War was imminent. Before putting himself at the head of his troops, to lead them onto the glorious path that he was going to trace from one extremity of Europe to the other, the First Consul made a new appeal for the intervention of Prussia. "What advantage," he wrote to Talleyrand, January 21, 1800, "would it be possible to draw from Prussia to accelerate the general continental peace or the partial peace with some one of the belligerent powers? What kind of notification could he be given that might entice him to back us more and more strongly?" That note tended to obtain from Prussia, for want of anything better, that she be so kind as to use her influence toward the reconciliation of Russia and France, which, since the reign of Catherine II had lived in a kind of state of permanent war. Communications on that matter had already been made by Talleyrand at the end of the previous year, but had been welcomed in Berlin only with vague responses. Instead of intervening with the Emperor Paul I, they confined themselves to transmitting coldly to M. de Krüdner, the Russian ambassador, the desire of the First Consul, whom they asked at the same time to specify frankly the claims that France would bring at the moment of concluding peace. Napoleon could not meet that demand under pain of committing a blunder; because what he wanted was that the powers meet, not to act on an ultimatum emanating from him, but to examine in concert the just requests of some and to reduce the excessive demands of others. On many occasions Talleyrand said to Sandoz-Rollin, the Prussian ambassador: "We have no political ambition, and that statement means much to your Court, which will know how to understand it. All that raised difficulties at Rastatt will do so no longer today." And, when his listener insisted on obtaining a precise declaration on such and such a point of the line of the Rhine, Talleyrand replied: "To affirm as we do that we have no ambition, that is to entice the belligerent powers to negotiate."

Some days later the First Consul himself said to the Prussian ambassador,

Would the king of Prussia wish to effect a useful reconciliation between France and Russia? I would commit myself then to make peace with Austria solely under conditions that will be judged the most appropriate for the maintenance of the general equilibrium. . . . In Germany I retain the line of the Rhine in the sense determined by the Treaty of Campo-Formio, setting aside all that which was appropriated by the former Directory. With the peace I shall again leave to the king of Prussia the choice of reentering into possession of his territories beyond the Rhine if he should prefer to keep them rather than exchange them. . . .

Also, when he saw that in consequence of the calculated slowness of Prussia he would accomplish nothing, when he judged that the hour of pacific hopes was passed, Napoleon, who had decided to take command of the army of Italy, declared to the Prussian ambassador that he declined for the moment the mediation of the King, formerly so much desired, and he added, "I shall now wage war, since it is forced upon me. They are mistaken, in Vienna and in Europe, on my pressing offers of peace; they are attributed to fear, to the penury of our resources and to the instability of the present government; a disastrous error of which they will soon be disabused. . . ."

It was the absolute conviction of Napoleon that neither France nor Prussia nor anyone in Europe would enjoy peace while there remained unchecked the cause of the evil which resided in London, where they were determined not to permit the existence of a great France capable of counterbalancing the influence of Britain.

A France humbled, diminished, reduced, according to the expression of Lord Auckland, "to a veritable political cipher," which would permit the English to develop alone, without competition, their fleet, their commerce, their industry; to subject the peoples to inaction, in order to be alone in supplying them with colonial provisions and products of their manufactures; to acquire thus a wealth more dangerous — as was soon to be seen, as can still be seen — for the repose of the world than all the armies of the continent united; this was the only price at which the British government consented to the reign of universal peace.

Napoleon was the man, was the Frenchman who did not willingly accept that humiliating and disastrous combination, and who opposed it tenaciously during fifteen years of war, for which the responsibility, whatever is said about it, falls on England, because she created all the coalitions and subsidized all of them. He was able to say very sincerely at Saint-Helena:

I always wanted peace with England, by all means reconcilable with the dignity of the French nation. I wished it finally at the price of all sacrifices that the national honor can admit. I had against England neither prejudice, nor hate, nor jealousy of ambition. What does it matter to me that England be rich and prosperous provided that France be like her? I did not contest with her the sceptre of the seas; I wanted only, I repeat, that she respect the flag of France on the seas as the emperors of Russia and Austria respect it on land.

There is no explaining any longer the history of that long period of wars by a sort of delirium of prosecution which maddened Napoleon each time that he thought of England. The madness of a single man is too easy a theme to define the cause of the greatest events, without counting the fact that it reduces to nothing the will of vigorous peoples, likening them to flocks of domestic animals who would be ready to exterminate themselves at the least gesture of a demented and fantastic being. That conception of the motives that Napoleon obeyed has been commonly admitted during three quarters of a century. That is no proof that it be not totally wrong, because there were excellent reasons for imposing it on public credulity. . . . A Talleyrand who had conducted almost all the diplomacy of the Empire, had written with his hand the sharpest letters against the rulers, had drawn up after the defeats treaties most humiliating to their self-esteem, who himself — like so many others — could not hope to be pardoned for such a past, if not by feigning to be the weak man, the muzzled servant, forced to obey the orders of a monstrous tyrant. And that legend, so oversimplified in truth, which permits rejection onto individual caprice of all the crimes perpetuated in Europe, has been propagated by England with the complicity of all the other nations.

Yes, that legend has involved all the nations: France first, influenced by her King Louis XVIII, who for twenty years as pretender had obtained from England everything, even the right to plot in England the assassination of Napoleon; then Austria and Prussia, Russia and the lesser states, Hesse-Cassel, Brunswick, Baden, Darmstadt, Portugal, Spain, Naples, Sardinia, all, great and small, each time the occasion was auspicious, had negotiated with the Cabinet of London against the French Republic or "the ogre of Corsica"; and, under the pretext that it was necessary to unite in order to defeat him, they have drawn millions and millions of pounds.

In seeing how the weakening, the dislocation of France entered into the desires of England, one begins almost to understand why the latter became more ardent in the struggle when she saw the Republic challenge Europe's provocations, organize her armies and make of the France that she wished diminished, enchained, a nation more independent, stronger, and greater than she had ever been. Logically, England

found herself even farther from her goal the day there appeared at the head of the government a leader, a sort of providential regenerator, who, in a short time, endowed France with a regular administration at home, with an unrivaled military prestige abroad.

What did England do when, six weeks after the 18 Brumaire, the First Consul, desirous of avoiding the intermediary of the implacably hostile British cabinet, wrote in his own hand to the King of England to ask for peace? Did she hasten, as good sense, the simple sentiment of humanity prescribed, to adopt that proposal in principle, to subject it to examination? Not at all. The British cabinet, basing the action on the text of the English constitution, on a law of etiquette, forbade the King to reply. The matter was taken before Parliament. One of the members of that assembly, Mr. Tierney, confronted with the obscure circumlocutions of the government, called on the prime minister to define his goal in a single phrase: "I do not know if I can do it in a single phrase," cried Mr. Pitt, "but I shall do it in a single word: security. Is security possible for England when our sole guarantee while negotiating would lie with this Bonaparte, sole organ now of all that is pernicious in the French Revolution?" Then, in conclusion, Pitt expressed his wishes in favor of the Bourbons, who would be enough occupied at home, repairing "ten years of revolutionary convulsions" and could not consequently, before ten years elapsed, meddle in external affairs. In that session of the English Parliament the respective sentiments of the two governments were illuminated. Napoleon said in his letter to the King of England: ". . . How could the two most enlightened nations in Europe sacrifice to vain ideas of grandeur, the benefits of commerce, internal prosperity, and the happiness of families?" In what manner did the British cabinet receive these generous advances? To justify the refusal of reply that it imposed upon the King, it aggravated its decision by explanations that it summed up literally in this phrase, "Reestablishment in France of the former dynasty which would assure to that country the possession of its former territory."

And, despite that kind of challenge that was thrown in his face, despite the insulting manner in which he was personally attacked, Napoleon did not diminish all his efforts toward the reestablishment of peace. He continued them even on the morrow of Marengo. After, as before, the victory he had his ear open to all propositions, however vague they might be, that came from the banks of the Thames, where, still faithful in 1801 to the system of 1789, "they did not cease," reports one diplomat, "to spend money in favor of the enterprises of Georges and of the Chouans." And what enterprises were they? One had just been seen on 3 Nivôse, when the infernal machine directed against the First Consul had killed fifty-six persons.

Despite everything, knowing that a more moderate ministry had succeeded Pitt, the First Consul tried all the means of conciliation before arriving at hostilities. A chargé d'affaires, Otto, had been sent to London under the pretext of settling the question of prisoners. In reality he had the more serious mission of preparing the way for a rapprochement, as his instructions specified. He was then pressed to make an explicit request for negotiations, and general views were exchanged between the two cabinets, after which it was possible six months later to bring together plenipotentiaries at Amiens to negotiate a definitive treaty of peace.

This is not the place to describe in detail the conferences, whose result was long uncertain, owing to the radical hostility that the English ministry encountered in an important part of Parliament; but, in order to be able to judge better on whom will rest the responsibilities for the succeeding wars, one ought to recall the ardent and sincere impatience of Napoleon when he awaited the result of the pacific negotiations in which England had finally deigned to participate; his gaze never left the road to Amiens; he counted the hours, the minutes; his thoughts followed the couriers from relay to relay, and he loaded them with tips so that they would accelerate the speed of their horses.

It is possible that he included in his fever of excitement the suspicion that perhaps the English would suddenly disappear and that he would see himself attacked by surprise on the coasts; the past invited him to be distrustful, the future will prove that he was not distrustful enough.

But very certain, in any case, and very categoric appeared his dispositions to conclude a specific arrangement. One is easily convinced when one follows by the hour the final negotiations. On March 8, 1802, he writes to his brother Joseph, who represents France at Amiens:

The last version of the English project for Malta is not far removed from ours. It is also easy to find a *mezzo termine* on the matter of the prisoners. I do not see now what can prevent the signing of the treaty today. If Lord Cornwallis is in good faith, the peace ought to be signed before the 19th. . . . I have conceded all that the English wanted.

On March 9:

I accept, although with regret, the formula, "The Sublime Porte is invited to accede to the present treaty. . . ." For the rest I give you all latitude to sign tonight. You will be in conference when you receive this letter; I don't think it will arrive before nine o'clock in the evening. . . . Do all that is possible to terminate the negotiations and sign. You will be careful to inform me, in your reply, if the courier arrived before nine o'clock, he having been promised in that case six hundred francs.

On March 11:

It is five o'clock in the afternoon, and I have not yet received the letter that you informed me you would send to me after your conference of yesterday and that I expected at midnight. . . . Please report to me twice daily, morning and evening, by two special couriers, all that you do and all that is said to you, because it is very evident to me that if, at the hour when I write, the peace is not signed or agreed to there is a change of system in London.

And it was always thus to the end; on March 24 he declared again on the version of an article in dispute: "The French plenipotentiary is authorized to proceed; he shall not delay by an hour the signature of the treaty on account of this article."

That is not, whatever one may wish, the language of a man who would prefer war to peace.

Master of the Mediterranean

EDOUARD DRIAULT

Edouard Driault (1864–1947) was a professional historian trained in the state university system, and he spent most of his career as Professor of History in the Lycée Hoche in Versailles. He wrote a number of books on Napoleon, and he was the founder, in 1921, of the journal of Napoleonic scholars, the *Revue des Études napoléoniennes*. He is remembered chiefly, however, for his five-volume work *Napoléon et l'Europe*, published between 1910 and 1927. Much of his writing is, in effect, a reply to Albert Sorel. Driault saw Napoleon as much more than a successor of Louis XIV and the Committee of Public Safety with his policies shaped by his predecessors, and he did not see England as the primordial and uncompromising enemy. The selection is taken from *Le Grand Empire, 1809–1812*, Volume IV of *Napoléon et l'Europe*.

NAPOLEON certainly did not have all at once a clear idea of his imperial future. Without doubt he did not want to be Emperor when he was still in the cradle. At exactly what moment did he have the idea? On the morrow of Rivoli, when he already appeared as the king of northern Italy, one of his officers reproached him for wishing to anoint himself with the holy oil; despite his perspicacity, that officer did not have a rapid advancement. Perhaps on the morrow of Brumaire, perhaps earlier, Napoleon thought of the conquest of Europe; but in the end the question is an idle one.

It is possible that he never had the clear resolve to succeed to the Roman emperors, although the name of Caesar came often to his lips, especially in the last years of his greatness.

Moreover, his education in history was mediocre. He did not know with scientific exactitude the character of the imperial sovereign power in Rome. In fact, he modeled his policy on circumstances; he profited from occasions; he developed his ambitions and his conceptions according to and in proportion to his victories. We never had the idea, although some have purported to have found it in our preceding volumes, to establish that, from the time of Brumaire, or from the time of the coronation, Napoleon had the firm wish to assure to himself the Empire of Europe. We studied step by

From Edouard Driault, *Le Grand Empire, 1809–1812* (Paris: Librairie Félix Alcan, 1924), 27–37, 416–418. Reprinted by permission of the Presses universitaires de France. [Editor's translation.]

step, in the first three parts of this work, with Marengo, Austerlitz, Tilsit, the development of his political thought. We did not see it from the beginning stiff and congealed in a mold that he then tried to fill with his conquests. We saw it grow, change, become more precise, made flexible by events, define itself little by little. . . .

Now that we have reached this date of 1810–1811, where some see the apogee of the Napoleonic Empire, let us take up again the stages already traveled in order to draw from its origins to here the curve of conquest and of imperial ambition.

Born in Corsica, issue of a Genoese family, Napoleon was a Latin; it need not be insisted upon; it is apparent to all, it was demonstrated long ago, and it is felt moreover that it was the fundamental character of his genius.

But, the Latin domain, the framework of Latin, or Greco-Latin, civilization, Rome being the daughter of Greece and Greece a province of Rome, was the Mediterranean.

Let us follow its contours on the north around Italy, Provence, Spain to Lusitania, or by Illyria, Macedonia, Dacia or Roumania, or on the south by the province of Africa, Cyrenaica or Lybia, Egypt, Asia Minor. We find here only the mark of Greek colonization or Roman domination. The Mediterranean is a Latin, or Greco-Latin, lake, *mare nostrum*, the Romans said. The only German who penetrated into it was Frederick Barbarossa, in the time of the crusade, and he was drowned on the way.

One must reread in the final pages of Mommsen, the grandiose picture of the Greco-Latin world, conquered by the Republic, organized by Caesar, the magnificent framework of the Empire, the cradle of all civilization, the seat of all historic grandeur.

The Barbarians passed by here, multiplied the ruins, burned Rome, destroying the temples and the palaces: pure vandalism, or jealousy of the marvelous countries that are not theirs.

The storm passed, Venice, Genoa, Mar-

seilles, Montpellier in the time of Jacques Coeur, were mistresses of the commerce of the Mediterranean, from the ends of the Black Sea, where they held all the heritage of Sidon, Tyre, Miletus, Phocaea, Athens, Alexandria, Rome. In modern times, up until now, as in ancient times, the heritage never left the family.

And the Germans stepping back from west to east, from south to north, toward their misty countries, are an illustration of one of the most striking laws of the history of recent centuries. They had, through fortunate marriages, won Spain, in the time of Charles V; the Hapsburgs reigned in Madrid for two hundred years. They imposed themselves on Italy by their imperial title. They were expelled from Spain by Louis XIV, who put the Bourbons in their place. Louis XV took for these Bourbons of Spain the largest part of Italy. They went little by little beyond the Alps. They still sought the South by way of the Balkans, by Asia Minor. Was that their place? These are today countries of Greek and Slavic predominance.

Napoleon wished to leave the Mediterranean neither to the Germans nor to the Slavs; he wished that it should be, that it should remain, entirely a Latin sea, and that is why he wanted it all for himself. It was for him part of the dream, of the melancholy dream, of the misleading dream.

From the time he was in the École militaire, evincing already an exuberant energy, he dreamed of offering his services to the Turks. Master of Italy in 1797, he immediately wanted the Ionian Islands, a road to the Orient, and that is why he destroyed the Republic of Venice. He then wrote to the Directory, "The islands of Corfu, Zante, and Cephalonia are more interesting for us than all of Italy put together." And he immediately sent General Gentili to take possession of them. "The island of Corcyra," he said also, "was, according to Homer, the country of the Princess Nausicaa. The citizen Arnault, who enjoys a merited reputation in literature, informs me that he is going to set out to plant the tricolor on the remains of the palace of Ulysses." At the time of the signing of the Peace of Campo-Formio, he already stated his ambition to the Austrian negotiator, the Count de Combenzl: "The French Republic regards the Mediterranean as its sea and wishes to dominate it."

He went, with what glory, beside the pyramids, and he prepared the resurrection of the Egypt of the Pharaohs; he retained the leading place there for France. He made himself master of Syria by taking Jaffa, Mount Tabor, the Lake of Tiberiade, Saint-Jean d'Acre. He thought of following in the footsteps of Alexander the Great, to take the road to India, or to return to Europe by way of Constantinople.

This was not permitted to him. He just missed being shut up in his conquest. With difficulty he returned to France through the English squadrons. He followed another career. But he kept his nostalgia for the Orient, the favorite country of his imagination. From 1803 onward he talked of returning to Egypt. He disputed Constantinople with the English and with the Russians. Until 1812 he thought of taking up again the conquest of Syria and of the valley of the Nile. . . .

He could not drive the English from the Mediterranean. They installed themselves in Malta, in the Ionian Islands. They made them the route to India. It was the beginning of their power on those privileged shores. Napoleon was, no doubt, cruelly hit by this, one of the sources of his hate for perfidious Albion, usurper of what he regarded as the best of his possessions. And he was obliged to build an Empire on the continent, an Empire less beautiful than that of the Mediterranean, than that of Caesar, and less durable. Hard and irreparable check to his ambitions, which were never to be successful in the Orient.

At least he established himself in Italy, at Rome, Genoa, Venice, Naples. He took possession of them through deeds of glory; in 1796, Montenotte, Lodi, Arcola; in 1797, Rivoli, Loeben, Campo-Formio. He established the Cisalpine Republic; he was like a proconsul in 1796–1797, "the Roman proconsul of the great epoch" writes Albert Sorel, "conquering statesman, organizer of the conquest and pacifier of conquered peoples. He is Julius Caesar in Gaul." "Italy," said the same historian, "was for Bonaparte what Gaul had been for Caesar, not only the road to power but the drill ground and the experiment ground for his Empire."

On his return from Egypt it is in Italy that he reestablished the fortunes of France, compromised by the Directory, and he consecrated his own at Marengo. He was president of the Cisalpine Republic, which he henceforth called Italian, evoking by a word the new Italy, to the acclamations of all the people if not of the princes; so is it true that all that he touched at once took form and grandeur in history and raised itself to new destinies. It is Italy that appeared.

Then he was King of Italy by the coronation at Milan. He took the iron crown of the ancient Lombard kings; as Charlemagne had done in restoring the Empire of the West, and the Ottos, founders of the Holy Roman Empire. At Austerlitz he destroyed the Holy Roman German Empire. From the Hapsburgs he took Venice, which he had just ceded to them, along with all her Mediterranean heritage, Dalmatia, Istria, the approaches to the ancient Illyria, another road to the Orient.

He took back Naples and Tuscany from the Bourbons. Everywhere he posed as the successor of the Bourbons, in Italy as in Spain. He even took Rome from the Pope, nominally to oblige him to join in the "continental struggle" against "the common enemy," England, mistress of the seas and especially of the Mediterranean; really because Rome is indispensable to the domination of Italy, because Rome is an essential element of the Empire, "the command post," says M. Lavisse. "You are sovereign in Rome," he wrote to the Pope in 1806, "but I am the Emperor!" "There is no Emperor of Rome," replied the Pope. Error: there was even a Roman Emperor.

Nevertheless, Napoleon put his indelible

mark on Italy. He was always in intimate communion with her, the native land of his family. He installed Elisa in Florence; she tried to revive there the memory of the Medicis; Caroline in Naples; Pauline Borghese in Rome. He prepared the transformation of the city of the Emperors; we shall look for the traces that he left there; they are very expressive.

He gave to all Italy the benefits of the Napoleonic Code. By civil equality as well as by special emancipation he awakened within her the sense of nationality. He created Italian patriotism in the scorching furnace of the Italian army, glorious on the battlefields of Austria and of Russia, of Raab and of Malo-Iaroslavets. He gave her her green, white, and red flag, whose green was his personal color, perpetuating his memory, the memory of his favors.

Henceforth Italy began to live; it was one of the foundations of the Empire, historically even more significant.

But it was necessary for him, on another side, in the heart of Germany, to strike directly at Austria, the fortress of the Holy Roman Empire, therefore the principal enemy of the Revolution, natural enemy of the new Empire born of the Revolution and of all the nationalities that, across Europe, in Austria herself, aspired to live on the appeal of the Revolution.

And beyond the Rhine, on the route prepared by the kings he crossed Germany through and through. Nevertheless, he was less at ease than in Italy; his clear Latin genius found itself uprooted in the territorial and political anarchy of the Germanies, and here he could make only imperfect experiments. At least he put a little order in the feudal disorder of Germany. He considerably simplified the map and regime, in the recess of the Diet of 1803, by the secularization of all the lands of the Church, except the archbishopric of Mainz-Ratisbon, by the suppression of almost all the free cities and of the nobility of the Empire. He thus prepared for the supremacy of the Protestants, and, among them, of the Hohenzollerns; it was the

germ, said Seeley, "of all the German Revolution of the nineteenth century."

His essential work, that which lasted the longest, which was the most efficacious, definitive, that was Austerlitz. There is the grandest glory of his reign. It would not be impossible to trace back to Austerlitz all the most characteristic traits of his historical role.

He here overthrew finally, after about ten centuries of existence, the Holy Roman Empire, enemy of peoples, the Bastille of Europe, barrier to the Revolution. Here without perhaps expressly wanting to, he gave the impulse to oppressed nationalities; he opened a new era in general history.

Then he started to found something in Germany. He established the Confederation of the Rhine. He formed a Kingdom of Westphalia, a colony of the French spirit. He undertook the organization of Germany, which left him totally at a loss, and he managed only to be exploited.

At least he resembled Charlemagne there more than elsewhere. Charlemagne had carried Christianity there, a means of introducing Germany into the civilized society of the time. He introduces the revolutionary doctrine, which doubtless will finish by introducing Germany into the civilized society of today. There was now another Charlemagne, with more splendor, more genius: "I did not succeed Louis XIV," he said, "but Charlemagne." He here took an imperial appearance already well characterized: "Napoleon," writes M. Lavisse, "did not believe himself confined to France; he did not localize his dignity; he is not the Emperor of the French; he is Napoleon Emperor."

And M. Lavisse sees an "intolerable anachronism" in that Empire that wishes to establish itself among the modern nations and at their expense. No. He fits exactly into the march of history; he destroyed the Holy Roman Empire, become an intolerable anachronism; he thereby assured the existence of the new nations; he conjured them up; he already made them live, under his tutelage at first because they were still fragile, and would be threatened with extinction on his fall.

"Whether it be good or bad," wrote James Bryce, "no one could doubt that in a sense France then and always represented the imperialist spirit of Rome more truly than those that the Middle Ages recognized as the legitimate heirs of its name and of its domination. . . . And it is the political character of the French, whether it be the result of five centuries of Roman government in Gaul, or rather the product of primitive instincts of the Gallic race, that can give them the right, better founded than any of those of which Napoleon took advantage, to call themselves the Romans of the modern world."

It is truly, in fact, the Roman Empire more than the Empire of Charlemagne, the Empire that sets in order the nations by removing them from disorder and barbarism, and that assures them fruitful peace and prosperity.

"The enemies of the imperial doctrine," writes the same historian, "cannot deny that it has already given and that it is still able to give the nations a sudden and violent access of aggressive energy, that it has often won the glory, if there is glory, that accompanies war and conquests; that it has acquired a better claim to respect by the facility with which it has formerly been able to become, in the hands of the Flavians and the Antonines and at the beginning of this century in the hands of Napoleon I, an instrument of reform of legislation and in government." Let us add here: an agency of social emancipation and political organization across all Europe.

Emperor and King of Italy, Napoleon was now, after Austerlitz, Emperor of the West, reigning over Italy and over Germany. In the place of the Holy Roman Germanic Empire he had established, and much more appropriately named, a Roman Empire of the West, of the French nation.

After Marengo, as after Rivoli, he could be called *Italicus*. After Austerlitz, the commemorative medal of the victory calls him *Germanicus*. He is also called *Ruth-*

enicus, la Russique, the conqueror of the Russians. He merited it even more after Friedland. Because he did not want to leave the East to the Russians. It was the final limit of his career, which brought him back to the Mediterranean, by the circuit of the continent.

At Tilsit he took back from the Russians the mouths of the Cattaro River, the Ionian Islands, Moldavia, and Wallachia, sent back all their ships in great haste into the Black Sea and into the Baltic Sea; he restored the Duchy of Warsaw, if not yet Poland, to bar their route into Europe.

At Erfurt, because of difficulties in Spain, he had to permit the Tsar to keep Moldavia-Wallachia. But by the Treaty of Vienna, of 1809, the Duchy of Warsaw was increased in size, and the government-general of the Illyrian provinces was organized under the direction of Marmont, the Duke of Ragusa.

The Eastern Question was clearly posed, and the rivalry of France and Russia in the region of Constantinople and of the eastern Mediterranean is the principal feature of the epoch at which we arrive on the morrow of Wagram.

One sees the wide expanse of the Empire at that date: France within her great frontiers, which are passed on the side of Italy, along the Tyrrhenian Sea, to below Rome, which is the capital of the department of the Bouches-du-Tiber; the Kingdom of Holland; the Confederation of the Rhine with the Kingdom of Westphalia; the Helvetic Confederation, the kingdoms of Italy, of Naples, of Spain; and beyond them two marches or frontier provinces, the Grand Duchy of Warsaw and the Illyrian provinces.

One does not need to look long at the map to see that that form cannot be definitive in the Emperor's thought. These two points, Warsaw and Laybach, one of which almost blots out Prussia, the other of which outflanks Austria by the south, point toward Eastern Europe and the Mediterranean.

The Empire was not at its apogee in 1810–1811, as is ordinarily said. . . . It was at that date still only at one stage of its development; it was still only a rough draft. It was far from realizing the thought of the Emperor, from having the form of which he dreamed. . . .

We shall not now penetrate into all the secrets of the Emperor. We cannot know exactly what he wanted, what he dreamed of. But we know what he did. We have the right and the duty to compare to one another his most expressive acts, the positive results of his policy, to explain them, to understand them, to find again their connections.

If we go back to the historical significance of the imperial title that we tried to analyze at the beginning of this volume, if we take up again in thought step by step the stages of the imperial conquest where were developed little by little by victory itself the political conceptions of the Empire, we are led to the top of that majestic curve, that is to the Kremlin of Moscow, to ascertain in the established facts, without arbitrary interpretation, a situation that can be expressed by some sure formulas.

The conquest of Europe was completed; all the powers of the continent were tied into the Napoleonic system; Russia was wounded in the heart in her sanctuaries of Moscow. It was, after twenty years of French victories, twenty years exactly after Valmy, peace assured by "lack of combatants"; who now, with Russia defeated, would again take up arms against France? Only there, and not on the eve of Jena, is it possible to claim that Napoleon wanted peace, or rather, that he held it, all his

enemies being vanquished. The temple of Janus was going to be closed.

Under the effort of the Emperor's genius, Europe was going to organize itself according to the principles borne of the Revolution; under protection for some time because still minors, the nationalities formerly subjects of the Holy Roman Empire were going to learn how to live by their own energy, conscious of their original virtues. It was the whole outlook of the continent transformed, a new period of universal history begun.

It was also the revolutionary doctrine thrust forever into all the countries crossed by the Grand Army; social privileges abolished, class barriers overturned, the great law of equality, foundation of all liberty, proclaimed in all the universe to open the modern era, the new times of which Napoleon will always, in the legendary centuries, be celebrated as the prophet.

And it pleases us to take up again here the comparison that history imposes between his work and that of the Caesars; they, too, had vanquished the aristocracy of the privileged, the government of the Senate; they, too, had founded their power on democracy. They were, or at least they pretended to be, the elect of the people, by the right of the sword; they, too, had assembled provinces, they had organized them, they had conceived of the Empire as the framework necessary for the emancipation of the lower classes and for the material prosperity of the world in peace. "I am," Napoleon then said to Maret, "I am of the race of the Caesars, and of the best, of those who laid the foundations."

Opportunist

PIERRE MURET

Pierre Muret (1875–1944) is known among historians chiefly as the author of a volume in the *Peuples et civilisations* series, *La Préponderance anglaise (1715–1763)*, published in 1937 after nearly twenty years of research and writing. Muret spent most of his career as a teacher in the Lycée Carnot in Paris, and he played a considerable role in the preparation for publication of the French diplomatic documents on the origins of the Franco-Prussian War and the World War of 1914. Among the earliest French historians to become interested in the historiography of Napoleon, he published in 1913 a review article on the many books that had appeared in the preceding decade and a half on Napoleon's foreign policy. This selection is taken from that article.

ONE OF THE first results of the researches and the writing of M. Driault is the condemnation of the historical fatalism of Sorel. This condemnation seems to us now to be justified by two series of conclusions that we have pointed out in the course of our analysis:

(1) If it is possible to establish a connection between the traditions of the *ancien régime* and the doctrine of natural frontiers that was imposed on the revolutionaries, it would not do to consider the Napoleonic conquest beyond natural frontiers as the logical consequence of the plans of the men of the Revolution. There is a personal element in the policy of Napoleon that the policy of the Revolution does not explain and that, on the contrary, appears to be in contradiction with it. What Sorel has clearly seen and established is that the acquisition of the natural frontiers supposed French action in Holland, in Germany, in Switzerland, in Italy and that that action had already been exercised earlier in the course of history. But did it necessarily suppose French conquest and domination? There is always some danger in history of fixing a policy in excessively absolute formulas. It is, nevertheless, permissible to say, that the tradition of the *ancien régime*, of which the members of the Committee of Public Safety of the Year III were the heirs, after the conquest of the natural frontiers, is that the influence of France beyond the natural frontiers ought to be extended by systems of alliances in which France would appear as a protecting power, and not as an oppressive power by a policy of intervention. . . . But the spirit of the Napoleonic policy was quite different. It reveals itself, in the course of M. Driault's book, as a policy of direct domination, which consents to compromise only with the hope of soon passing the limits that circumstances have been able momentarily to impose upon it.

(2) But it might have turned out that the necessities of the struggle against a Europe ceaselessly belligerent would have imposed on Napoleon that idea of domination beyond the natural frontiers, and such indeed was the thought of Sorel. It is, in our opinion, one of the most interesting results of the works of M. Driault to give us very strong reasons to believe that it was not thus. Sorel in fact had studied the

From Pierre Muret, "Une conception nouvelle de la politique étrangère de Napoléon Ier," *Revue d'histoire moderne et contemporaine*, XVIII (1913), 369–370, 378–380. Reprinted by permission of the Société d'Histoire moderne. [Editor's translation.]

negotiations of the Consulate and of the beginnings of the Empire only from above and especially to discover, while simplifying them excessively, the same elements of conflict and the same causes of defeat as in the earlier negotiations. If one analyzes them in detail, or if one considers the various solutions that could have resulted, one finds oneself led to recognize, with M. Driault, that beside the extremely varied solutions of Napoleon, could be found quite practicable combinations, quite varied elements of negotiation.

The analysis that we have made of the books of M. Driault has permitted us to establish the Napoleonic responsibility, because it has permitted us to establish that in the most important negotiations the Napoleonic diplomacy would have been able to adopt other courses than those that it chose. . . .

Universal supremacy and domination, these are the realities that in our opinion the imperial formulas conceal. However, M. Driault does not accept such an interpretation of Napoleonic policy. "The term universal domination," he writes in *La Politique orientale de Napoléon*, "is vague." It leaves around the name of Napoleon that misty glory "that enchains the multitude and pleases it, it does not penetrate with sufficient clarity the imperial secret, it does not permit a definition of his policy." That one can oppose the imperial theory to the universal domination theory, to find in one the precision lacking in the other, we do not believe, and we have just stated the reasons that incline us to mix them. But what is interesting to retain is the objection that M. Driault formulates here; that by one of these theories — and we would say by the other as well — one does not penetrate the imperial secret. It leads us, indeed, in terminating our study to pose a question, which all the recent historians of Napoleon in France supposedly resolved and which, in our view, is by no means resolved. Is it certain that the Napoleonic policy had a defined objective? Did there exist a grand Napoleonic plan susceptible of being pre-

cisely stated? Before seeking the explanation of the imperial secret, can one not ask himself if what we know of the intentions and of the various projects of Napoleon permits the existence of a secret?

We shall observe first that having an objective implies choice, subordination of other projects to a well-defined plan, discipline imposed on action. But Napoleon — it is at least the impression that we have drawn from the works of M. Driault — never wished to choose. Simultaneously, in all directions, he conducted the most diverse enterprises. The most illustrative example of it that can be given is that of his diplomacy after the peace of Amiens. Commercial and economic supremacy over the English, organization of a barrier of French client states beyond the natural frontiers, establishment of a Napoleonic Italy, Oriental and Mediterranean ambitions; Bonaparte intended to sacrifice none of these plans to the others. Between the establishment of French domination, beyond the natural frontiers and the struggle against England, of which the cause is especially economic, commercial, and Mediterranean, he could choose, and, indeed, one has the impression in reading M. Driault that the English peace had prevented continental war and inversely that a policy intended to rally the continental powers could weaken England and deprive her of the support of the continent. But Napoleon refused to make this choice. And this is not an exceptional fact in the history of Napoleonic policy. Considering in M. Driault's volumes the chapters devoted to Napoleonic expansion after Pressburg, one will come to analogous conclusions.

On the other hand, if Napoleon did not consent to sacrifice certain of his ambitions to the success of other ambitions, he also had the least apt mind to understand the necessity of compromise. This is not to say that he had not been in certain circumstances a consummate diplomat, nor that he had not in certain cases limited his pretentions. But — and M. Driault established it with an abundance of proofs — he consented to moderate his ambitions only momentarily, with the idea of soon passing the stage where he stopped. It had never been part of his plans to take into account the interest or ambitions of others. The study of his relations with Prussia concerning the Confederation of North Germany, of his relations with Russia concerning the Eastern Question, bring us convincing evidence on this matter.

Finally, from the analysis that Sorel has made in *L'Europe et la Révolution,* and from that of M. Driault, can be gathered the way that all the questions which were to create in Napoleon's mind the most gigantic conceptions are connected. The necessity of an active policy on the right bank of the Rhine resulted from the conquest of the natural frontiers; the formation of a French Germany beyond the Rhine led to the humiliation of Prussia that posed anew the question of Poland. Similarly, the partition of Venice posed, along with the question of the domination of the Adriatic, that of Constantinople. Also similarly, the policy of the continental blockade preceded from the necessities of the struggle against England. From these various statements results the conclusion, it seems to us, that one does not need to assume a definite plan; it suffices to place the man with his tendencies of mind and of character opposite the problems that, stage by stage, are posed to him in more and more breadth and complexity. That does not diminish, however, either his responsibility, or the colossal value of his effort to impose his solutions on Europe.

Thus the conclusion to which in the last analysis we come is that the Napoleonic policy is explained, not by a determined plan, but by a state of mind, and that the state of mind of Napoleon, given the repercussions of the questions that are posed to him and the resources at his disposal, was to lead him to the most grandiose and the least defined conceptions of conquest and of domination.

III. MILITARY GENIUS OR REVOLUTIONARY GENERAL?

Rival of Hannibal

ADOLPHE THIERS

Thiers considered himself an expert in military affairs, and he perhaps wrote with particular relish the portions of his book devoted to Napoleon the warrior. Certainly he left no doubt about his judgment of the Emperor's military abilities.

THE FRENCH of 1789 had two sentiments in their hearts: the chagrin at having seen France decline since Louis XIV, which they attributed to the frivolities of the court, and indignation against the European powers, which wished to prevent their reforming their institutions on the principle of civil equality. Thus the entire nation ran to arms. The old royal army, although deprived of a notable part of its officers by the emigration, sufficed for the first encounters, and under a general, Dumouriez, who for fifty years had wasted his genius in vulgar intrigues, fought victorious battles. But it soon melted in the fire of that terrible war, and the Revolution sent to replace it masses of men who became infantry. Cavalry, artillerymen, engineers cannot be made from men drafted in haste, but in an essentially military country, which has the pride and tradition of arms, foot soldiers can be made of them. These foot soldiers, incorporated in the half-brigades remaining from the old army, bringing to it their audacity, taking from it its organization, first attacked the enemy as sharpshooters, then threw themselves on

him in a mass bayonet charge. In time they would learn to maneuver under the eyes of the European armies most skilled in maneuvers, those trained in the school of Frederick and of Daun; in time, too, they would furnish artillerymen, cavalrymen, engineers, and acquiring the discipline that they at first lacked, retaining the audacity and the mobility of their first glow, they soon constituted the first army of the world.

It was not possible that the powerful sentiment of '89, combined with our secular military traditions, should give us armies without also giving us generals, that our infantry, having become skilled in maneuvers like the best German armies, and in addition more eager, more alert, more audacious, should not exercise an irresistible influence on those who commanded it, and it effectively pushed forward Pichegru in Holland, Moreau, Kléber, Hoche, Jourdan in the middle of Germany. But while it formed generals capable of competently commanding an army, it was to form not two but one who would be capable of directing at once all the armies of a vast empire, because moral movement is like

From Adolphe Thiers, *Histoire du Consulate et de l'Empire* (Paris: Paulin, Lheureux et Cie., 1845–1862), **XX**, 757–763, 767–776. [Editor's translation.]

physical movement, imposed on several bodies at once, it moves each of them distances in proportion to their volume and their weight. While Pichegru, Hoche, Kléber, Desaix, Masséna were the product of that national movement, the master of them all revealed himself at Toulon, and that master whom the universe named, was the young Bonaparte, trained in the bosom of the schools of the old regime, in the most scholarly of arms, that of artillery, but full of the new spirit, and joining to his own audacity, perhaps the greatest that has inspired a human soul, the audacity of the French Revolution. Endowed with the universal genius that makes men fit for all employments, he had, moreover, one characteristic that was peculiar to him, the application to study the ground or the map, and the penchant to seek here the solution to the phenomena of politics as well as the problems of war. Ceaselessly sleeping on maps, which military men do too rarely and which they did even less before him, he meditated continually on the configuration of the soil where war then raged, and to these profound thoughts joined the dreams of a young man, saying to himself that if he were the master he would do this or that, would push in such and such direction the armies of the Republic, not at all suspecting that he would one day be master, but feeling some indefinable ferment which would soon pierce the soil and spurt out as a rich spring. Engaged in these solitary meditations, he had understood that Austria, having renounced the Low Countries, was vulnerable only in Italy, and that it was there that the war must be carried to make it decisive. Talking ceaselessly of these dreams to the directors, of which he was the clerk, almost tiring them, he is first named commandant of Paris, and then, Schérer letting himself be defeated, general of the army of Italy. Scarcely arrived at Nice, the young general sees at a glance that he need not force the Alps, and it suffices *to outflank them,* as he put it with so much wisdom. As a matter of fact the Piedmontese and the Austrians guarded the *col de Montenotte,* where the Alps come down to rise farther away under the name of the Apennines. He makes a threat toward Genoa in order to draw the Austrians there, then in a single night forces the *col de Montenotte* when the Piedmontese alone remain on guard, pushes them back, in two battles hurls them back on Turin, wrings peace from the King of Piedmont, and hurls himself on the Po in pursuit of the Austrians, who, seeing that they were tricked in letting themselves be drawn to Genoa, hurried to return to protect Milan. He crosses the Po at Plaisance, enters Milan, hurries to Lodi, forces the Adda, and stops at the Adige, where his transcendent mind shows him the true frontier of Italy against the Germans. A less profound genius would have run to the south to seize Florence, Rome, Naples. He does not think of it. It is with the Germans that Italy must be disputed, he tells the Directory, it is against them that position must be taken.... He decides therefore to remain in the north, and with the same genius saw that the Po has a course too long to be easily defended, that the Isonzo, too advanced, is always exposed to be outflanked by the Tyrol, that the Adige alone can be victoriously defended, because immediately after it emerges from the Alps at Verona that stream falls into the marshes of Legnago, and placed on this side of the Tyrol it cannot be outflanked. The young Bonaparte establishes himself then on the Adige, reasoning as follows: If the Austrians want to force the Adige by the mountains, they will necessarily pass by the plateau of Rivoli; if they want to force it by the plain, they will put themselves either before Verona or toward the marshes in the environs of Legnago. From that moment he must place the mass of his troops in the center, that is, at Verona, leave two detachments on guard, one at Rivoli, the other towards Legnago, reenforce alternatively one or the other according to the direction that the enemy takes, and remain imperturbably in that position, making the siege of Mantua a kind of pastime between the various appearances of the Austrians. Thanks to that profundity of judgment, with 36,000 men, reenforced by scarcely 15,000 in the course of the war, the young Bonaparte resists all the Austrian armies, and in eighteen months winning twelve battles, more than sixty lesser combats, taking more than 100,000 prisoners, crushes Austria and wrings from her the definitive abandonment of the line of the Rhine to France, plus the general peace.

Certainly, one can run through the pages of all history, and nothing equal will be seen there. The general conception and the art of combat, all are found in a degree of perfection never encountered elsewhere. . . . To await the enemy before Verona; if he presents himself directly to repel him, thanks to Caldiero's choice position; if he turns to the right toward the low country to go to fight him in the marshes of Arcole, where numbers are nothing and value is everything; if he descends on our left by the Tyrol, to receive him on the plateau of Rivoli; and the master of two roads — that at the bottom of the valley that the artillery and the cavalry follows, that of the mountains that the infantry follows — first to throw the artillery and the cavalry into the Adige, then to take prisoner the infantry, deprived of the support of the other arms, to take 18,000 men with 15,000 — there is the art of warfare. And to do all that at twenty-six years, to join all the profundity of mature age to the audacity of youth has, we repeat, nothing equal in history for grandeur of conception combined with perfection of execution.

All the rest of the career of General Bonaparte is marked by the same traits: transcendent understanding of the object at which one must aim in a campaign, and profound ability to profit from the terrain where the circumstances of war bring you to battle; in a word, equal superiority in general movements and in the art of giving battle. . . .

In Italy Napoleon had been a subordi-nate general, reduced by limited means; in Austria, in Prussia, in Poland, he was the general, chief of state, having at his disposal the resources of a vast empire, giving to his operation the full scope of his conceptions, and overthrowing Austria in a day, Prussia in another, and Russia in a third, and all that at distances unprecedented in the conduct of war. He had been in the first case the model of the subordinate general, he was in the second the model of the all-powerful and conquering general. Here no longer those limited movements around a fortified place, those classic battles where the cavalry was on the wings, the infantry in the center; the movements have the proportions of the empire to be attacked, and the battles the exact physiognomy of the places where they are to be fought. The battles resemble, while surpassing, that at Leuthen; and as for the movements, they have quite a different scope from those of Frederick, running breathlessly from Breslau to Frankfurt-sur-l'Oder, from Frankfurt-sur-l'Oder to Erfurt without ever striking the decisive blow that would have ended the war. Not that one should not admire the activity, the perseverance, the tenacity of Frederick, very worthy of his designation of great! It is nevertheless true that the French general, adding the audacity of the French Revolution to his own, studying the principal features of the soil as was never done before him had achieved a range and a precision of movement such that his blows were at once sure and decisive and in a way without appeal. The art, one can say, has achieved its final limits.

Unfortunately that prodigious success was to corrupt not the general, each day more consummate in his art, but the statesman, to persuade him that all was possible, to lead him soon into Spain, soon into Russia, with armies weakened by too rapid replacement, and across difficulties ceaselessly growing, first by distance, which was no less than that from Cadiz to Moscow, then by the climate that was by turn that of Africa or of Siberia, which forced men to pass from 100 degrees above to 20 degrees below zero, extreme differences that animal life could not stand. Amid such recklessness, the greatest, the most perfect of captains must succumb!

Also many judges of Napoleon, who, without ever being severe enough on politics, are much too severe on his military operations, reproached him with being the general of successes, not that of reverses, of knowing how to invade, of not knowing how to defend, of being the first in offensive war, the last in defensive war, which they sum up in this phrase, that *Napoleon never knew how to retreat.* That is, in our view, an erroneous judgment.

When in the intoxication of success, Napoleon moved distances like that from Paris to Moscow, and in weather where the cold fell 20 degrees below zero, no longer was retreat possible, and Moreau, who commanded the admirable retreat from Bavaria in 1800, would certainly not have led the French army from Moscow to Warsaw intact. If disaster like that of 1812 occurred, that was no more than one of the alternatives of war that sometimes oblige you to advance, sometimes to retreat; it was as if a whole structure crumbled on the head of the audacious man who had wished to raise it to the skies. The armies, pushed to the last degree of exaltation to go as far as Moscow, finding themselves suddenly surprised by a deadly climate, feeling themselves at an immense distance, knowing that peoples were in revolt on their rear, fell into a desolation proportionate to their enthusiasm, and no longer could any power keep them in order. It was not a practical retreat that the chief did not know how to make, it was the edifice of a universal monarchy that crumbled on the head of its daring creator!

But one would not be a general if one were not a general in adversity as in prosperity, because war is such a succession of happy and unhappy alternatives, that he who cannot face up to the one and the other could not command an army two weeks. Now, when Napoleon, attacked by the Austrians in November 1796, in the middle of the fevers of Mantua, having scarcely 10,000 men to put in the line, threw himself into the swamps of Arcole in order to annul the power of numbers, he gave proof of a firmness and a fertility of mind in difficult circumstances that certainly have few equals. When in 1809, at the time when a series of great political blunders had begun, he found himself at Essling driven to the Danube, deprived of all his bridges by an extraordinarily high water in the river, and fell back to the Île de Lobau with an imperturbable *sang-froid,* he demonstrated no less solidity in reverses. Without doubt the resistance at Essling itself was the prodigy of Lannes, who died there, of Masséna, who would have been dead there if God had not made him as lucky as he was tenacious; but the firmness of Napoleon, who, in the middle of an aroused Vienna, discovered resources that all our demoralized generals no longer saw and the firm and patient plan by means of which the victory was brought to our flags at Wagram. That firmness, so much admired by Masséna was indeed Napoleon's, and that moment certainly offers one of the most grandly and most gloriously passed crises of war of which the history of nations has preserved the memory.

Finally, to give immediately the most decisive proof, the campaign of 1814, in which Napoleon with a handful of men, some worn out, others never having been under fire, held off all Europe, not by beating a retreat but by profiting from the mistaken movements of the enemy to make him retreat by terrible blows, is yet another example of the fecundity of resources, of presence of mind, of indomitable firmness in a desperate situation. Doubtless Napoleon did not wage defensive war, like most generals, withdrawing methodically from one line to another, defending the first, then the second, then the third, and succeeding thus only in gaining time, which is not to be disdained but which does not suffice to terminate a crisis happily; he waged defensive war like offensive war; he studied the terrain, tried to foresee how the enemy would act, to surprise him in making a blunder and to crush him, which he did against Blücher and Schwartzenberg in 1814, and which would have assured his salvation if all around him, men and things had not been worn out.

If he was not properly speaking the general of retreats because he thought like Frederick that the best defense was offensive, he showed himself in unhappy wars as great as in happy wars. In the one as in the other he maintained the same character of vigor, of audacity, of promptness to seize the point where it was necessary to strike; and if he succumbed, it was not, we repeat, the military man who succumbed in him, it was the politician who had undertaken the impossible, in wanting to conquer the invincible order of things.

In the organization of armies Napoleon was no less remarkable than in the general direction of operations and in battles.

Thus before him the generals of the Republic distributed their armies in divisions composed of all arms — infantry, artillery, cavalry — and reserved in addition an uncommitted division, made up like the others, in order to parry unforeseen attacks. Each of the lieutenants fought an isolated battle, and the role of the general-in-chief consisted of aiding the one among them who needed it. One could thus avoid defeats, even win battles, but never those crushing battles after which a power was reduced to laying down its arms. With the person of Napoleon, the organization of the army corps was to change, and to change in a way to leave in the hands of him who directed everything the means of deciding everything.

In fact, his army was divided into corps of which the infantry was the base, with a portion of artillery to sustain it, and a portion of cavalry to enlighten it. But independently of the infantry of the Guard, which was his habitual reserve, he kept for himself masses of cavalry and artillery, which were like a lightning bolt that he held to throw at the decisive moment. At Eylau the Russian infantry appearing immovable, he threw upon it sixty squadrons of dragoons and of cuirassiers, and this opened in it a breach that was never closed. At Wagram, Bernadotte having let our line be pierced, he stopped the victorious center of the Archduke Charles with one hundred cannon and reestablished the battle that Davout ended, in winning the plateau of Wagram. It was for that that he had formed two reserves, the one of heavy cavalry, the other of heavy artillery, which in his hand were the club of Hercules. But the hand of Hercules is essential to the club, and with a lesser general than Napoleon, that organization would have had the inconvenience of often depriving skillful lieutenants of special arms that they would have known how to turn to account, in order to concentrate them in the hands of a chief incapable of using them. Also almost all the generals of the republican army of the Rhine, accustomed to act in an almost independent manner, which allowed them to combine a sufficient portion of all the arms, regretted the loss of the former composition, which comes back to saying that they regretted a state of things that had left them more importance on condition of diminishing the results of the whole.

But organization does not consist solely in good distribution of the various parts of any army; it consists in recruiting it, in nourishing it. In that respect, the art that Napoleon deployed to carry the conscripts from their villages to the banks of the Rhine, to those of the Elbe, of the Vistula, of the Niemen, collecting them in depots, watching over them with extreme care, letting them almost never escape, and thus leading them by the hand to the field of battle, that art was prodigious. It consisted of an infallible memory for details, in a profound discernment of negligence or infidelities by subordinate agents, in a continual attention to repressing them, in an indefatigable strength of will, in an incessant labor that often filled his nights when the day had been passed on horseback. And despite all these efforts, the roads were often covered with disbanded soldiers, but which attested only one thing, it is the violence done to nature in moving men from the banks of the Tagus to those of the Volga!

To these so various tasks of the general-in-chief it is often necessary to join another, it is that of subjugating the elements, to cross snow-covered mountains, broad and violent rivers, and sometimes the sea itself. Antiquity has left for the admiration of the world the crossing of the Pyrenees and the Alps by Hannibal, and it is certain that men have done nothing more grand, perhaps even as grand. The crossing of the Saint-Bernard, the transportation of the army of Egypt through the English fleets, the preparations for the Boulogne expedition, finally the crossing of the Danube at Wagram are great operations that posterity will admire no less. The last, especially, will be an eternal subject of astonishment. The difficulty consisting on that occasion of going to seek out the Austrian army across the Danube to bring it to battle, and to cross that broad river with 150,000 men in the presence of 200,000 others, who awaited us to throw us in the flood, without being able to avoid them by moving above or below Vienna, because in the first case one would be too far advanced and in the second one would have to pull back — that difficulty was surmounted in a marvelous manner. In three hours 150,000 men and 500 cannons had crossed in front of the stupefied enemy, who thought to attack us only when we had put foot on the left bank, and when we were able to resist him. The crossing of the Saint-Bernard, as extraordinary as it was, is far from equaling the crossing of the Alps by Hannibal; but the crossing of the Danube in 1809 equals all the operations attempted to vanquish the combined power of nature and of man, and will remain a phenomenon of profound foresight in planning, and of calm audacity in execution.

Finally one would not say everything on the military genius of Napoleon if one did not add that to the most diverse qualities of intelligence he joined the art of dominating men, of communicating his passions to them, of subjugating them as a great orator subjugates his audience, sometimes restraining them, sometimes throwing them forward, sometimes finally reanimating them if they are shaky, and always finally keeping them in hand as a skillful horseman keeps a difficult horse in hand. He lacked nothing of mind or character necessary to be the true captain, and one can sustain the proposition that if Hannibal had not existed he would probably be without equal.

Genius

MAXIMILIEN YORCK VON WARTENBURG

Maximilien Yorck von Wartenburg (1850–1900) was a member of the Prussian General Staff, and at the time of his accidental death in 1900 he was regarded as one of the rising men in the Prussian army. Highly interested in Napoleon's military career, he was moved to write a book on the subject by his conviction that the appearance of many studies of Napoleon and the publica-

From Maximilien Yorck von Wartenburg, *Napoleon as a General* (London: Kegan Paul, Trübner & Co., 1902), II, 442–453.

tion of his correspondence made possible "a complete judgment" of the Emperor's military abilities. The resulting book, *Napoleon as a General*, was originally published in German and was soon translated into French and English. The English edition was aimed at the market of British army officers, who, the publisher and translator thought, could learn much from it.

WE HAVE hitherto followed the Emperor step by step in his military career, and we will now halt, in order that, from a distance, we may place him in the right perspective, and obtain a clear impression of him. We find, first, that the foundation of his strength lay in his clear perception of actual facts, in his practical intelligence, of which Carlyle said: "The man had a sure, instinctive, ineradicable perception of actualities, and based himself upon facts, as long as he had any basis at all." In the time of his strength and his successes, he said of himself, that "he was of all men the greatest slave of a pitiless master, of the calculation of events and the consideration of the real meaning of hard facts."

But with this practical intelligence there was combined the wide-reaching, prophetic glance of a boundless power of imagination. We saw that this quality is necessary to a military leader if he is to rise to the highest flights; and yet in this very quality lies the germ of the reason why the greatest military geniuses are not destined to achieve permanent results. "Napoleon, although living entirely in a world of ideas, never actually realized that there was such a world, and refused to believe in its actual existence, while all the time zealously striving to realize it." In the same way as Napoleon's practical intelligence led him to overrate the importance of the numerical element, as opposed to the moral element in war, so his power of imagination degenerated into wilful self-deception. This latter predominated more and more as his dreams were fulfilled, and as his power and empire rose higher and higher, he thought at last that nothing was impossible to him. "You say, 'It is impossible'; there is no such word in French." "Even in trivial things, when

perhaps some course was represented as impracticable, it seemed ridiculous to him that any one should say, 'I cannot . . . etc.,' and he never abandoned his own idea until the impossibility became absolutely evident. So much had good fortune spoilt him."

Thus the former "slave of hard facts" was transformed by the over-luxuriance of his imagination into the most insolent and absolute despot; and the fact that he deceived not merely others, but himself also, became the source of his failures. "He became an apostate from his old belief in facts, and began to believe in things which had no reality." Events were to be as he wished them to be; and if they were not so, he declared the hard fact to be simply untrue, thinking such a declaration sufficient to attain what was impossible and to undo what had been done. It is a proof of an absolutely deranged mind, that he presented to the eye-witnesses and participators in the great disaster of 1812, only one month after they had left Russia, the following description: "The reports which reach me from all sides, confirm the opinion that the Russians on the Beresina considered themselves as lost, and that Victor would have beaten them, had it not been for the unfortunate affair with Partonneaux, just as we beat the admiral; that Kutusov's corps was entirely annihilated, and that he never dreamt of marching to Vilna, but remained at Minsk."

We may here remark, that the great men of the Latin or Slav races frequently combine, with their great qualities, a certain charlatanism, which is foreign to the great men of the Teutonic race. Neither Gustavus Adolphus, nor Frederick the Great, nor the Archduke Charles gave evidence of this, nor even Wallenstein or Charles XII. But Napoleon could not avoid tricking out his successes, real and great though they were, with a few tinsel additions; they were not only to be brilliant, but they were also to appear so. Proofs of this may be found in all his bulletins; and of his proclamations he said himself: "There was a touch of charlatanism in them, though of the highest order."

We must allow, however, that this to a certain extent is quite true; indeed Napoleon himself said, "impressions are more than half the battle." Is there a man who has not in his own life often experienced the truth, that awkward or silent merit is outweighed by pretensions which are only calculated to attract notice, so that what at first was mere pretension becomes ultimately tangible success? We have only to quote, as an example, Clausewitz's opinion of Kutusov: "Thus the frivolity and charlatanism of this clever old rascal turned out, as a matter of fact, to be of greater use than all Barklay's straightforward dealing could possibly have been."

The men of the Latin or Slav races act thus, not only because they therein follow the inner promptings of their own nature, but above all because they meet the demand of their people; and the fact that they feel themselves thoroughly in harmony with them, and fulfil their expectations in this respect also, is of the greatest assistance to them. Gambetta and Skobelew are good instances. We must never forget that success is the first and only thing for a military leader; and whenever history undertakes to judge a man merely as a general, it must judge of his qualities from this point of view alone. We shall thus understand why merit, which knows not how to cut a brilliant figure or make a brave show, is less successful, and therefore actually inferior, compared with that which knows how to advertise itself, even by means of charlatanism. Of what avail was it, I will not say, to Moreau, but to Moreau's country, that he waited modestly, until he was sought out, whilst his rival pushed him on one side and placed himself at the head of affairs, by employing all possible means, both those of pretence and those of reality?

And in the same way as we note in intellectual Napoleon the rare combination of cool reason and glowing imagination, so we note in him as a soldier a peculiar combination of two qualities which are but rarely granted to the same leader. Military history, indeed, shows us, on the one hand, leaders of troops who, gifted with great power over the minds of their subordinates, are in their proper sphere as actual leaders and organizers of battles at the head of their men, but who are wanting in the abstract power of combining strategical movements on a map. On the other hand, it shows us individuals who possess this gift of strategical combinations in an eminent degree, who can form within themselves a wonderfully clear picture of the largest dimensions, but who become confused by actual contact with the troops themselves. Thus Delbruck quotes Brandt's criticism of Clausewitz: "On the battle-field he would have been quite out of place. He lacked the art of carrying the troops along with him. This was not merely due to bashfulness or embarrassment, but to a want of the habit of command. If one saw him among the troops, one noticed in him a certain want of ease, which disappeared as soon as he left them." A Blücher, on the other hand, and a Suvorov, are brilliant examples of the former quality; and inasmuch as in warfare strength of character outweighs clearness of insight, it is not a matter of surprise that their fame is greater. We know that Gneisenau possessed the second of these two qualities, but had no opportunity to prove his possession of the first; whilst the opposite was the case with Skobelev. Still with both these men we have grounds for assuming that they did possess the other quality which is needed to make a true general. In the case of Lee, however, it seems that he was endowed more with the power of strategical combinations than with power over human nature. Stonewall Jackson and Stuart were evidently in this point his superiors, and his complements.

But in Napoleon we see also both these

qualities combined in the highest degree. Few men like him could carry away the common soldier by the charm of their personality. He knew how to inspire his masses with a devotion that defied death. "His appearance electrified the troops. Although the major portion of Ney's corps consisted only of quite young conscripts, who probably were this day for the first time under fire, yet rarely did any wounded pass him without crying out: Vive l'Empereur! Even the mutilated, who would in a few hours be the prey of death, paid him this homage." He himself was moved by the sight of this emotion, of which he was the cause, and his own enthusiasm was kindled by this eagerness for battle, which he kindled in others. "Whenever his senses were affected by the sight of a large mass of troops, he always experienced a vivid impression, which reacted upon his resolution."

His superiority in the seclusion of his study, in his labours with compass and map, was no less great; and in this consists his importance in the study of the art of war. He is not merely the great practical man of action, whose deeds are full of instruction for us; he is also the great master of theory, whose words teach us. Many of his letters are actually treatises, which might find a place in any theoretical work on strategy; and we find the expressions: base, line of operations, front of operations, lines of communications, etc., as frequently in Napoleon's letters as in Jomini's treatise on the art of war. Thus, for example: in 1806, his letter to his brother Louis, which contained the development of his plan of campaign; in 1808 his memoranda to Joseph, in 1813 his notes on the situation after Dresden and before Leipzig, and then again his letters to Dejean, about the value of fortresses and on operations in connection with fortresses. It is because the great principles of strategy were so plainly illustrated by his deeds, and because he acknowledged and emphasized their existence in his own words, that the history of Napoleon's wars are so instructive to us. "All the plans of Napoleon's fourteen campaigns are in harmony with the true principles of war; his wars were bold, but methodical." This severe regularity in his whole conception and practice of war renders Napoleon's strategy a most instructive example for us.

Empirics are in the habit of discounting all endeavours to gain a knowledge of the true principles of war through the study of instructive treatises, by saying that war is a living entity, the parts of which cannot be learnt, and which cannot be confined to any set of rules. We readily admit that war is a living whole, and that to wage war successfully, one must master it as a whole. But just as the physician, who desires to influence the living human organism by his remedies, must begin by dissecting the parts of the dead organism and studying the principles and the composition of the individual parts, in order to recognize the vital functions of the whole, so is it with the art of war. No one has ever maintained, with respect to medical science, that theoretical study is useless, and that a physician could at once begin with practice; indeed whoever did so, would be considered a bungler; and yet as regards the art of war, people are to be found who declare theoretical study to be actually hurtful. In medical science, although every individual case of sickness has its special features, yet may be treated according to general rules, so also in the art of war, although every situation may offer something new, yet after all will fall under general rules. Finally, as only that physician is a true master of his art, who, having all the general rules entirely in his grasp, employs them not with slavish uniformity, but modifies them according to the nature of each individual case, so only that military leader will attain to perfection in the art of war, who, while fully acquainted with the domain of theory, employs its principles according to the nature of the given case. The rational employment of general principles marks the difference between the genius of the true artist and the lack of freedom of the mechanic who is dominated by rigid rules, and the bungler, who despises all rules and denies their justification.

For art is art. Call him not artist yet,
Who never deeply thought on art!
To grope is useless. Knowledge sure and true
Alone to great success can lead.

In this respect, therefore, I trust, this attempt of mine to analyze the mind of a great general, may be considered to be justified. The Emperor himself was so firmly convinced that there existed a theory of the art of war, and that it could be expressed in definite words, that once, in speaking of the difficulties of carrying on war, he said: "if some day he had the time, he would write a book, in which he would formulate its principles in such a detailed manner, that they would be capable of being understood by every soldier, so that war could be learnt, just as any other given science."

But, above all, Napoleon's importance in the history of war lies in his originality. Through him the value of masses has come to be recognized as contrasted with the art of strategy in the 18th century. In old days the tactical value of a body of troops seems to have occupied, in the opinion of generals, a higher place than its numbers. It is true, even in our days, that the efficiency of troops is of great importance, and all efforts in the direction of increasing this efficiency are of the highest value; still strategy, as founded by Napoleon, is characterized by basing all its plans upon the calculation of one's own and the enemy's numbers and upon the appreciation of masses. And the employment of masses leads necessarily to the principle, that the highest aim of strategy is the destruction of the enemy. Consequently in Napoleon's strategy and in that of our days, which is based upon his, the real goal of all operations is the enemy's army, and the consummation aimed at is battle. Finally, with his principle of the employment of masses, Napoleon paved the way for wars in which whole nations take part, for the formation of armies based upon universal military service.

It is of great value to us, that in the case of Napoleon, circumstances permitted a great military genius to attain its utmost development. Caesar was assassinated on the threshold of his dominion, and though we may assume that in him the general had, by that time, given place to the statesman, yet we have no actual proof of this conjecture. Alexander died young, and we may doubt whether his military genius would have been sufficient to maintain for any length of time the empire he had conquered. To Hannibal the highest sphere of action was never vouchsafed.

It is true, circumstances have an overwhelming influence. Only the end of the last century, only the France of those days, could have produced a Napoleon. In the case of Gneisenau, whatever was Napoleonic in his nature could not come to maturity on account of the pressure of external circumstances. If, in the case of Lee, we admire much that is Napoleonic in the conception and execution of his plans, we must after all acknowledge that circumstances were with him wholly different, and another and very different future was in store for the modest chief of the academy of Lexington than for the haughty prisoner of St. Helena.

Still the predominant factor of our fate lies in our own personality. "Men's passions decide their fate, they themselves are the result of their individual positions." It is true, circumstances block many paths for us, which in accordance with our natures and gifts we might pursue, yet there ever remains to us a choice of many directions; we are not inevitably compelled by fate to follow one, and only one road; and even in Napoleon's career we may note many a parting of the ways, on occasions where he had the unfettered opportunity of framing his own future.

But if we see that a military genius of the stamp of Napoleon's is undoubtedly ready, and indeed bound to be ready, to pursue Napoleonic methods, wherever circumstances do not absolutely preclude such a course, this fact shows us that, for the lasting welfare of a state, sound military institutions are even more necessary than one military leader of genius. Rome had no general worthy to vie with Hannibal, and Rome had its Cannæ, but its military institutions withstood even that crushing blow, and finally gained the victory. Napoleon had no equal as a general, yet Waterloo brought his empire to the ground, when his genius, weakened by age and sickness, had deteriorated by self-conceit, and the France of those days did not possess any military institutions capable of withstanding the catastrophe.

We recognize consequently, that Napoleon became the greatest of generals because he voluntarily renounced becoming a great monarch; indeed, wherever the highest goal is aimed at, a certain singleness of aim, a one-sided development, is inevitable; and therefore, the further we advance in our study of Napoleon as a military leader, the oftener our judgment of him can be compressed into those words of Jomini: "The French general's manœuvre might be pronounced correct, strategically speaking, the statesman's operation was only bold."

Still we must note that this one-sidedness of development is of advantage only to the individual success of a man; it is of harm as far as the permanence of his work is concerned; and we understand why the state founded by the richer and more philosophic nature of Frederick enjoyed a healthier development than that founded by the Emperor Napoleon, as is described in the final paragraph of Taine's great historical work in these mournful words: "No more beautiful barracks have ever been built up, nor any more even and ornate in appearance, or more satisfactory to shallow minds, or more acceptable to the ordinary human intellect, or more comfortable for narrow-minded egotism, or better kept, or arranged in a more cleanly and altogether better

manner, or more fit to overawe the mediocre and lower sides of human nature, whilst allowing the loftier sides of human nature to be stunted and corrupted." Rigid one-sidedness may be of advantage to one human being, the life of a nation needs a more supple many-sidedness.

But in this one-sidedness of direction, in order to reach the really highest goal, an energy that knows no bounds must be displayed, which knows no repose of satiety, in fact such an energy as we saw embodied in Napoleon, and which might be seen in him in the first years of his activity. Even in 1797 that saying, characteristic and true of all the highest and Caesarean natures, was applied to him: "I know of no other goal for him except the throne or the scaffold."

Although his empire itself crumbled into dust, yet his military acts remain a lofty ideal for the soldier. Whoever now enters that vaulted hall under the dome of the Invalides, and looks at that simple, dark red sarcophagus of porphyry which bears no name, but only the laurel wreath of mighty battles, will think with marvelling admiration, and, if he is a soldier, with veneration, of that unruly, quarrelsome child; of that taciturn officer, always buried in thought, rarely sociable, often insubordinate; of that excitable general, always active, bold in resolution, unwavering in execution, ambitious and passionate; of that conqueror of genius, never satisfied, always despotic; of that egotistical Emperor, disregarding the future, despising men, a fatalist, who had become incapable of any sacrifice of his own personal comfort; of that ill-tempered prisoner of St. Helena, wanting in veracity and stretching out his hands convulsively into empty air, trying to grasp the lost empire of the world; of the corpse of him who was the greatest military genius. Every soldier will appreciate the justice of his own words: "I aimed at the empire of the world; who in my place would not have done the same?"

First in War?

ALBERT L. GUÉRARD

For more than half a century as teacher, scholar, and writer Albert L. Guérard (1880–1959) exposed myths and stereotypes in American views of France and offered his own, often unorthodox and always provocative, interpretations. Born in Paris and educated in France, he came to the United States before the outbreak of war in 1914, became an American citizen, and spent his life teaching in American universities, notably at Rice and Stanford. He was a prolific writer, and he produced many books on history, literature, and criticism, including brief biographies of both Napoleon I and Napoleon III. His *Reflections on the Napoleonic Legend*, one of his earlier publications, is a critical comparison of the legend with the established facts of Napoleon's career as Guérard saw them as well as a study of the legend's genesis and growth. In it he takes a fresh and unfettered look at Napoleon as a military commander.

LET us examine this God of War, then, in the cold, clear light of Voltairean common sense, brushing aside, for a moment, the prestige which usually paralyses our reasoning. It is a dangerous undertaking for a layman to comment on Napoleon as a leader of armies. Chateaubriand made himself exquisitely ridiculous by his famous declaration: "Napoleon's military glory? It is torn away from him. He knew how to win battles; apart from that, there is no commonplace general that is not more skilful than he." Technicians in the art of war, for a century, have based their doctrine upon the study of his campaigns. Generals who professed to be the disciples of Napoleon have won victories over generals who, to be sure, were likewise the disciples of Napoleon; so, whatever the issue, his prestige was secure. It would be as foolishly presumptuous for the non-specialist to pit his opinion against that of the experts, as it was presumptuous to challenge from without the authority of schoolmen, theologians, and diplomatists. The reader may be sure that we shall not venture upon technical military ground. We are perfectly willing to accept on faith that the Italian campaign in 1796 and the campaign of France in 1814 are the unsurpassable masterpieces of military genius. In so far as war is an art for its own sake, the practitioners thereof are alone qualified to have an opinion. But if war be a means to an end, if it occupies a definite place in a larger scheme of things, then even the man in the street may see its broad results and judge of its success. It is therefore just as legitimate for a student of history to discuss Napoleon the general as it is to discuss Colbert the administrator and Metternich the diplomatist. Even in the question of Napoleon as the God of War, we are justified in pointing out the element of legend. Miraculous as his career may be, it has artificially been made more miraculous still. And a greater miracle has thus been sacrificed, because it was not incarnated in a single hero.

The common conception is that France would inevitably have succumbed, had not Napoleon's genius saved her on the brink

From Albert L. Guérard, *Reflections on the Napoleonic Legend* (London: T. Fisher Unwin, 1924; New York: Charles Scribner's Sons, 1924), pp. 36–52. Reprinted by permission of Ernest Benn, Ltd.

of the abyss. It is this vague and persistent impression that we must challenge. In 1793 the situation of France was desperate indeed. The whole of Europe was in coalition against her; one-third of her territory was in open rebellion against the Central Government. Throughout the part of the country controlled by the Republic a large proportion of the population was in sympathy with the foreign aggressors and with the rebels. Even in the capital, royalism, driven underground, was ceaselessly intriguing. In Paris there ruled the most amorphous Government: the collective, irresponsible dictatorship of an assembly hopelessly divided against itself, and in constant danger of being invaded by the mob. The republican leaders were sending one another to the guillotine, because, forsooth, they were "exaggerated" or else "indulgent." Scientists were executed, like Lavoisier, or hunted to death like Condorcet. Trained officers had deserted almost in a body, and were carrying arms against the Convention. Those who had remained at their posts were under suspicion, and several were sent to the scaffold. The volunteers called in 1792 behaved as raw recruits will almost invariably behave, whatever may be their personal courage and devotion: at the first attack they fled in a panic, shouting: We are betrayed, and shot their officers. It seemed as though only a miracle could save France and the Revolution. And the miracle did happen.

France was saved partly by the mutual jealousy and distrust of the Powers banded against her. She was saved because vast flocks of the vultures left her to swoop upon Poland, an easier prey. But she was saved also by a miracle of energy and organization.

To meet an unheard-of emergency, a new kind of war was evolved. To the small, highly trained forces of the Prussian type were opposed levies on an unexampled scale — fourteen armies and twelve hundred thousand men. The veterans of the old regime and the recruits of the new were amalgamated, blending experience with enthusiasm. Discipline was restored, intelligent and rigorous. Officers were picked out from the ranks or from civil life. Hoche, a sergeant, found himself at the head of an army at twenty-six. It would have been suicidal to match these untrained hordes, these improvised officers, against the masters of the craft at their old game, learned and cautious, of strategic chess. So the young revolutionary giant, whilst Austrian and Prussian champions were smilingly watching for the next move, grabbed the old chess-board and smashed it on their venerable heads. Revolutionary tactics, revolutionary strategy, guided the revolutionary army. And the victory was not one of sheer numbers or brutal courage alone. Science was pressed into service. Quicker processes provided arms and gunpowder for the eager masses. The semaphoric telegraph of Chappe, the captive balloon, gave miraculous wings to the young Republic. The war was a crusade of fraternity and justice; and, as in the glorious group of Rude, the spirit of the Marseillaise hovered above the marching hosts.

The result was the greatest epic of war that the world had yet seen. In two years the barefooted armies of the Republic had conquered on all frontiers. By 1795 the back of the coalition was broken. Prussia and Spain were suing for peace. France had won the ancient frontier of Gaul, the left bank of the Rhine. She had won it by the triumph of her arms, and she won it again by the justice of her cause; for the next twenty years the Rhinelanders were faithful members of the French family, faithful even in the hour of trial, at a time when others wavered, who had lived for five centuries under the sceptre of the Capetians. In two years the Convention had won what the Kings had dreamt of for half a millennium — what Napoleon was to lose again after draining Europe of her purest blood.

The most miraculous element in that military miracle is that it is anonymous. That is why English or American imagination so obstinately refuses to be fired by it. The central character, the "Organizer of

Victory," the man who called into existence the fourteen armies of France, and hurled them against reactionary Europe, Lazare Carnot, is no fit hero for a legend. There is nothing flashy about that modest, hard-working captain of Engineers, capable, no doubt, of risking his life on the battle-field in order to encourage wavering troops, but condemning himself, as a rule, to the obscure travail of co-ordination in his Paris office. So he who invented modern warfare, and made Frederick II almost as antiquated as Alexander of Macedon, he who wrested victory from rout, he who forged the instrument for the great conqueror, is, beyond the frontiers of France, all but forgotten. We must add that he would have been the first to disclaim any unique share in the collective effort; he, his immediate associates, the Prieurs, Cambon, Jean Bon Saint André, the scientists, the young generals, the peasants in tattered blue coats and wooden shoes, all were the servants of a cause — a cause greater than France herself. So they had their reward and passed into oblivion.

Once more, the critical years, the miraculous years, were 1793, 1794, 1795. By that time a tradition had been formed, a generation of officers had been tried and trained. The heroic mob that rushed helter-skelter to defend "the Fatherland in danger" had become a complex, accurate fighting machine; Europe had learned to respect the ragged army of democracy. And by that time what had Napoleon done? At first he had shilly-shallied between the cause of Corsican independence and Jacobinism in France; he had intrigued, obscurely and unsuccessfully; he had served the Robespierres, and disowned them after their fall. He had at last had a chance to play a creditable but secondary part in a minor operation, the Siege of Toulon. Meanwhile Hoche, his elder by a few months only, had already commanded in chief. Of course there is no discredit for a youth of twenty-six in the fact that he had only attained the rank of brigadier-general. The point is that Napoleon did not play a leading or

even an important part in the dramatic recovery which changed France from a country on the eve of dissolution to the greatest military power in Europe. All that he performed later with the instrument that Carnot had prepared was not so wonderful as the creation of the instrument itself, and the success with which it was used before the Treaty of Basel.

In October 1795 we find Napoleon Bonaparte, distrusted by the Government, in obscure technical employment at the War Office. A Royalist plot against the moribund Convention broke out. The best generals were at the front. Others, whose services might have been available, were under suspicion. For the decrepit Revolutionary giant was steering a devious course between Jacobinism and Reaction, and no one knew for certain who were his friends or his foes. Barras, the principal personage in the Thermidorian regime, was appointed General-in-Chief of the Interior. He needed a military man as his instrument, and he needed him at once. The young Corsican general happened to be on the spot, and too obscure, it seemed, to become a danger. So he was selected. The resistance of the Royalists was feeble, and the famous "whiff of grapeshot" near the Church of St. Roch finally dispersed them. Carlyle descants on that incident as though the military had never been called upon to quell an insurrection. There had been many such whiffs before, and there were to be not a few more in the troublous annals of nineteenth-century France. But this one started echoes which reverberate to this day.

Napoleon had his chance at last; he was entering history, although it was through a back door of no savoury repute. For he had become the right-hand man of that clever and sinister character, Barras, who took pride in his nickname, "le roi des pourris" — the rottenest of the rotten. The humble position of Bonaparte at any rate may be gauged by the fact that it was considered a great boon for him to receive the hand of Josephine, one of the Merry Widows of the Thermidorian carnival, and the discarded mistress of the all-powerful Barras. The young officer of fortune fell sincerely in love with the fading Creole beauty: and in her marriage portion was found the command of the Army of Italy.

Carnot had prepared a gigantic plan of campaign against Austria. Whilst Moreau and Jourdan were to reach Vienna by striking north of the Alps, Bonaparte was to march upon the same capital through the valley of the Po. In the mind of the great strategist it seems that the Italian campaign was destined to remain secondary, perhaps a mere diversion on a large scale. The economy of the plan was upset by the personality of the leaders: the Austrians had their best general in the north, the French theirs in the south. So the northern campaign was a failure, the Italian one a series of triumphs, and Bonaparte became in popular estimation not only the foremost of the French generals, but a worker of miracles. The present writer knows too little about military art fully to appreciate the wonderful series of manœuvres, bold and swift, through which the young commander defeated five armies outnumbering his own. But its general lines are eloquent enough even to the merest layman. One feels that a difficult art has reached, in 1796 and 1797, its point of perfection. No other campaign gives us the same æsthetic pleasure.

It may seem futile and ungracious to suggest reservations. Unfortunately, that is what the critical student of history must train himself to do. The campaign justifies the most thoroughgoing admiration for Napoleon as a strategist: it does not justify the belief that his ability was miraculous or even unique. The only Austrian general who had learned anything about the new methods of warfare was engaged north of the Alps. Alvinzi, Kalkreuth, Würmser, were honourable Austrian warriors, true to the tradition of that country, which was to remain always a little behind the times. The Austrians were slow in realizing the shifting importance of the two campaigns, and they sent into Italy reinforcements

which Napoleon was able to defeat in detail. He destroyed five armies without a general, and then dictated peace to a general without an army. In appraising the merits of a victory, it is necessary to consider against whom it was won, as well as by whom. The blunders of his opponents and his own genius were both necessary elements in his triumphal progress. Moreau and Jourdan had a different task to accomplish.

Furthermore, in comparing the failure of the northern campaign with the success of the southern one, we are apt to forget that only one of the Republican commanders, Jourdan, proved unequal to his task. Jourdan, whose career had been creditable rather than brilliant, was badly beaten. Moreau, left without support, doomed as it seemed to utter defeat, managed to extricate himself through a retreat which has remained a classic — a retreat in which he not only kept his army intact, but inflicted repeated punishment upon his pursuers. As soon as the troops were reorganized, Hoche and Moreau opened a new campaign, and their initial operations were as brilliant as anything that Bonaparte himself had to show. But the Preliminaries of Peace, signed at Leoben, arrested this magnificent beginning, and the casual reader still thinks of Napoleon, at twenty-seven, as in a class by himself.

There is another aspect of the Italian campaign, which, as a lover of France, we should prefer to leave untouched. But it is a symptom which cannot be ignored. War, from 1792 to 1795, had, on the French side, a missionary tinge. This gave it a chivalric appeal rare in history, an appeal to which fair-minded Germans have not remained indifferent, from Goethe in 1792 to Karl Vossler in 1921. That spirit was changing. For that change Napoleon was not responsible. It was not his fault if the generals, instead of being citizens arming for the spread of the Rights of Man, had become, most of them, professional soldiers, eager for promotion and pay, even for "graft" and loot, in the service of a corrupt and predatory Government. But Napoleon did nothing to check this spirit of brutal ambition. Far from it; true to his principle that no tool was to be despised when it could serve some purpose, he cynically appealed to it. His ringing proclamation on assuming command is worth remembering: 'Soldiers, you are ill-clad, ill-paid: I am going to lead you into the richest plains in the world, where all of you may find glory and fortune." The captain of a pirate ship could find no better words to encourage his crew.

The Italian expedition was not only a model of tactics, strategy, diplomacy, and good administration: it was also an example of systematic exploitation, of looting on a magnificent scale. In this domain the conquerors of Rumania in 1917 were the apt pupils of Napoleon. The Home Government needed it; there were moments when the cartloads of gold sent by General Bonaparte were the only thing that stood between the Directoire and immediate bankruptcy. Napoleon nursed or created grievances against Powers which could afford to pay, such as the Pope or the Venetian Republic. It was a universal game of grab. But Napoleon liked efficiency even in thieves. Officers were allowed to "collect" only according to their rank, and contractors had to provide the army with suitable goods. The General-in-Chief himself was noted for his abstemiousness; he was already playing a deeper game. It was enough for him to know that there were in Europe plenty of talents and loyalties to be bought. He gambled heavily on the sordid side of human nature: where had "incorruptibility" led Robespierre and Saint-Just? And for many years he was not disappointed.

We may add that among his loot were a number of masterpieces, wherewith French museums were enriched until 1815. This again is an Italian trait: some of the *condottieri* were art lovers and art collectors. A true barbarian would not have appreciated the value of old paintings and statues. Pekin has seen a whole brood of petty Napoleons twice in a generation, in 1860 and in 1900.

His next military venture was a piece of romanticism which should have proved his undoing, and yet served his Legend almost as potently as his Italian victories. He took a French expedition to Egypt: perhaps there were some Machiavellians in high places who were delighted to see him go, and whose secret desires very nearly came to pass. The conception was grandiose and baseless. No doubt Egypt is the pivot of the ancient world, the strategic key to the East, as Saint Louis and Leibniz had realized centuries before Lord Beaconsfield. But the conquest of Egypt, by a small army, and without the control of the sea, was bound to be futile. And so it proved to be. Napoleon was hemmed in on the banks of the Nile. He tried to invade Syria, and was checked by one of his old schoolmates. The East was barred against him; all that Bonaparte could hope was to found in Egypt a local military domination, similar to the very Mameluke regime that he had overthrown. He was already coquetting with Islam, and we might have had a turbaned Napoleon-Bey in Cairo instead of an Emperor in Paris. Baffled in his dream of rivalling Alexander, Napoleon quietly abandoned his army to its fate and sailed for Europe. Kléber maintained himself heroically; but he was assassinated, and his successor, Menou, had to capitulate. No fiasco could be more complete, and, for the general who deserted his post, more shameful. The expedition had later a magnificent by-product: it made Egyptology a French science for several generations, and led to the deciphering of the hieroglyphics. This, however, would hardly be accepted as an excuse in a military court.

Yet the fame of Napoleon was enhanced by this expedition. The prestige of the East, as he had rightly anticipated, gave him a halo. "Great reputations," he would say, "are made only in the East." Successful or not, the Egyptian raid was an adventure, a romance. It means something in the history of France that her soldiers should have fought in the shadow of the Pyramids, from whose heights, as Napoleon said, forty centuries were looking upon them.

His failure was distant, unsubstantial, poetic, redeemed by colourful episodes; the failure of the men who had to carry out the foolhardy policy of the Directoire was immediate, and fraught with tragic consequences. In two years, the Government, in its rake's progress, had forfeited all the advantages of Campo-Formio. France was once more thrown upon the defensive; the immense front might break at many points; and Russia, the untried champion, vast and terrible, had at last joined the coalition. The memories of the Italian triumphs stood luminous against that murky present. Bonaparte to the rescue! He alone could save France.

The curious thing is that even in our own days the general public are under the impression that he did. In his absence, all went from bad to worse; he returned, and victory changed sides. Yet the actual facts are accessible — nay, familiar to all. Victory had changed sides already. Masséna had broken the back of the coalition at Zurich. Suwaroff, defeated, and, in addition, resenting hotly the punctilious pride and the pedantic procrastination of his Austrian allies, was retreating, with no thought of coming to grips with the French again; Brune had compelled the Duke of York to capitulate at Bergen. It was not Bonaparte's return that altered the face of events; yet the man who had left his army behind was acclaimed, and is still acclaimed by posterity, as though it were he and not Masséna who had conquered at Zurich.

The tide had turned, but peace was not won. Masséna's stubborn resistance in Genoa enabled Bonaparte, now First Consul, to gather a new army, which, with wonderful skill and secrecy, he took over the Alps. This second Italian campaign culminated in the Battle of Marengo. Here, again, plain facts do not quite tally with the legend. Napoleon actually lost the

Battle of Marengo, and Melas had already left the battlefield to spread broadcast the news of his triumph — the only time in history when an Austrian general acted with something approaching haste. Desaix, without orders, rushed in the direction of the cannonade. Everyone remembers the famous words: "It is three o'clock. The battle is lost. But we have time to win another." That second battle was won, and Desaix was killed. Destiny was kind to her favourite Bonaparte. She had removed Hoche, stricken with consumption, Kléber, assassinated in Cairo, Desaix, shot on the battle-field — the only generals, as Lord Rosebery remarks, that Napoleon ever praised wholeheartedly. It was reserved for Moreau to bring the coalition to terms through his victory at Hohenlinden: an obscure intrigue was soon to drive that last possible rival, at first to America, and finally into the ranks of France's enemies.

Under the Convention miracles were accomplished, but Napoleon was still obscure. Under the Directoire and the Consulate, he had forged to the front rank, but remained only *primus inter pares,* with such peers as Hoche, Kléber, Desaix, Masséna, Moreau. His chief advantage over most of them was his craftier and more ruthless ambition; his decisive advantage over the three noblest is that they died and he lived.

Marengo marks the end of Napoleon's normal career as a general in free competition with other generals. After that time no comparison was possible; the dice were too heavily loaded in his favour. Against his foreign rivals he enjoyed the tremendous advantage of being sole military and political ruler of a united Empire, whereas they were the instruments of a loose coalition. Before the Allies had time to put their heads together, agree upon a policy, and divide the prospective spoils, he was already knocking insistently at the gates of their capitals. It is evident that if Austria, Prussia, Russia, supported by England, had acted in concert in 1805, Napoleon's genius would have had an immensely harder task to accomplish. We know from recent experience the full value of unity of counsel and unity of command. Thanks to a superior degree of such unity, the Germans maintained themselves for nearly four years against overwhelming odds. When unity of command was at last accomplished, their doom was sealed, as inevitably as Napoleon's doom was sealed as soon as the Allies worked with one purpose.

With other French commanders, Napoleon would brook no comparison, even remote. Of the older men, Masséna, "Victory's favourite child," was the most formidable. Napoleon secured the grudging allegiance of the victor of Zurich by allowing him to loot to his heart's content, or almost to his heart's content, for Masséna, like his imperial master, was insatiable. But he was careful never to give him a chance commensurate with his genius. Brune was never forgiven for his victorious campaign in Holland. His memory remains smirched with the unproved allegations that Napoleon allowed to be whispered against him. In 1806 the main body of the French army shattered the forces of Prussia at Jena; but at the same time, at Auerstaedt, Davoust was defeating an enemy outnumbering him. Of these twin battles, Auerstaedt is the more meritorious; but Napoleon scooped all the glory, and Davoust was henceforth kept in honourable but subordinate employment. The Polish crown, which seems to have been dangled before his eyes, came to nothing. It was not until 1815, when most of Napoleon's marshals had deserted him, that he gave Davoust's talents full scope; and even then he used him as an organizer, not as a fighter. In 1809, when the Emperor was held in check near Vienna — the decisive victory of Wagram makes us forget how critical the situation of the French had been — the British made a descent at Walcheren, in Holland. Fouché organized the national guards of the Empire, appointed Bernadotte as their commander, and said: "Let us prove to Europe that, although the genius of Napoleon may give lustre to France through his

victories, his presence is not necessary for repelling the enemy." He was successful, but he had committed the one unpardonable sin: he had hinted that France could exist without Napoleon, and he was summarily dismissed. A burly new Chief of Police, introducing himself to his subordinates, boasted: "I can lick anybody on my force." A still burlier officer stepped forward and said: "You can't lick *me*." The Chief eyed him for a moment, and then waved him aside: "You are no longer on my force."

The result of this method was the surprising mediocrity of Napoleon's personnel compared with Carnot's. The older men were losing heart; a new generation of courtiers and bureaucrats was waiting to step in their shoes. Napoleon was supreme for fifteen years; the number of men he discovered and advanced is extremely small. Ney and Soult are, perhaps, the most prominent of the purely Napoleonic generals. Ney was brave and Soult was skilful, but neither of them could compare with Moreau, Masséna, Desaix, Kléber, and Hoche.

Winter and Providence have been blamed for the failure of the Russian campaign — Napoleon's infallibility remaining above discussion. Providence is inscrutable, but winter might have been foreseen. And if the Napoleon-worshipper offers as a further excuse the fact that his vast army was loose, heterogeneous, grumbling, with disaffected elements, and even germs of active treason, we may reply that the Grand Army of 1812 was of Napoleon's own making, and that he had thought it adequate for a campaign which was not forced upon him. The truth is that he had weeded independence and moral courage out of his staff, unselfish enthusiasm out of the rank and file. Worn out by twenty-five years of feverish activity, he had become sluggish, rousing himself from his drowsy spells only to give vent to fits of peevishness. He had acted for ten years the part of an Oriental tyrant; the vices and even the infirmities of an Oriental tyrant were creeping upon him.

We find in this campaign the limit, not of his luck merely, but also of his genius. He never had led before — no one had ever led in modern times — an army of six hundred thousand men. It would have taken a creative genius to meet the new conditions, and Napoleon's genius was not creative. He excelled in using standard tools; invention he scorned. He turned down Fulton, and was satisfied with the artillery of Gribeauval. He handled a horde of six hundred thousand men with the mental equipment which had served so well in his Italian campaign, and the mass proved unwieldy in his hands. He had never paid any adequate attention to supplies from the base. He was a careful administrator, and he had the welfare of his soldiers at heart; but it was his principle that war should be self-supporting, that the army should live on the country in which it was operating, and that the heads of subordinate units, down to the squad, could be trusted to shift for themselves. This worked admirably in Lombardy and in Germany; those lands were rich, and not fanatically hostile to the French. But the system, or absence of system, had already brought him within an ace of disaster in the Polish campaign of 1807; it is only by a polite fiction that Eylau is still mentioned among French victories. In 1812–1813 that tremendous herd of reluctant men found itself in mid-winter in a hostile, devastated country, without a commissariat. For the hardships of the famous retreat Napoleon's lack of foresight alone was responsible.

He woke up, and was himself again, for the German campaign of 1813; it was in the course of that campaign, by the way, that he ordered everything destroyed on the right bank of the Elbe, "down to the last fruit tree" — a precedent which the Germans did not forget in 1916. The campaign of France in 1814 is by common consent even more marvellous than that of Italy in 1796. There again he defeated in detail several armies larger than his own. But the Allies had learned their lesson: they pressed on relentlessly, and, whilst gaining battles,

he was losing the war. Fighting for dear life, his raw levies fired with patriotism and steadied by his veterans, on ground familiar to many of his officers, he was under the best conditions for surpassing his greatest achievements. We were rather surprised, therefore, when we read a lecture by Marshal Foch, then Lieutenant-Colonel, on the Battle of Laon (March 1814). The great professor of strategy, who was to disprove so conclusively the alleged antinomy between *teaching* and *doing,* analyses the causes of Napoleon's failure with pitiless objectivity: it is a "lesson" at the close of manœuvres, nothing else. And the Napoleon he evokes is not the demi-god drawing fresh vigour from the sacred soil upon which he is fighting: it is a Napoleon who hesitates, is poorly informed, and too sluggish to find out for himself the true situation of affairs; a Napoleon who allows himself to be engaged into a battle by the action of irresponsible lieutenants. The consensus of historians is that the Waterloo campaign was mediocre. Napoleon's former dash seemed utterly lacking. When his generals saw his sickly pallor on that ominous morning of June 18th they had a vision of disaster. The absence of worthy lieutenants was tragically felt; but it was Napoleon who had wanted to be served by men like Grouchy.

What are the conclusions of this rapid survey? That Napoleon was not a great general? We trust that no reader will accuse us of such an absurdity. The quality of his army, the divisions and the slowness of his enemies, do not suffice to explain all his triumphs: men like Jourdan had held the same trumps in their hands, and lost the game. Napoleon was a virtuoso of war. He did not create his instrument, the new army; he did not write the tune — swift, massive attacks on vital points: both had been made ready for him by Carnot. In his twenty years of prominence, in his fifteen years of supremacy, he never produced a new method, a new weapon, or a new man. But he was a performer of supreme skill, and it is the performer, not the composer, who enjoys the plaudits of the public. Like most great masters of technique, he did not look forward. So, when he had an unprecedented situation to meet, in the Russian campaign, he broke down. We may wonder whether, even with railroads and wireless at his disposal, he would have been able to fill the place of Marshal Foch: ten million men to command, five million of them actually on the battle-line, four great allied nations to co-ordinate, several Parliaments eagerly watching him, and, opposing him, an enemy immensely superior in armament, training, and leadership to the coalition of 1814.

"He took France bankrupt, torn by factions, threatened with invasion; and, through the sheer magic of his genius, he made her the sovereign power in Europe." There is little doubt, in the mind of whoever reads dispassionately the well-known facts of the case, that this conception is a myth. Shall we say: "He sprang into prominence only after France, defeating all her foes, had reached the frontier of the Rhine, and when she had an army unexampled in numbers, discipline, and morale. So long as the impetus of the Revolution lasted, so long as his enemies were hesitating, divided, trammelled by antiquated military doctrines, Napoleon was able to carry on, in splendid style, the work of Lazare Carnot. When he had dried up all the founts of enthusiasm, when he had thoroughly discouraged initiative and fostered sycophancy, when his opponents had at last mastered the principles of the new strategy, he fell, and left France weary, body and soul, distrusted abroad, and much smaller than when he assumed power."

Militarist

ALFRED VAGTS

Alfred Vagts (1892–   ) was born in Germany and educated at the universities of Hamburg and Munich and at Yale. He is the author of books on international relations and military history, the most recent being *The Military Attaché* (Princeton University Press), published in 1967. The selection that follows is taken from his *A History of Militarism.* Fundamental in this book is the author's distinction between "the military way" and "militarism." The former is "limited in scope, confined to one function, scientific in its essential qualities." Militarism, on the other hand, connotes "a domination of the military man over the civilian, an undue preponderance of military demands, an emphasis on military considerations, spirit, ideals, and scales of value. . . ." Napoleon, he concludes, developed into a militarist.

THE CIVILIAN dreamers of the Revolution, who sought to create a new social order in France, may have imagined that the mass armies designed to defend the Revolution at home and abroad would docilely serve the lawyers and ideologues at Paris to the end. If so, they were quickly disillusioned. When the Directory em-

From Alfred Vagts, *A History of Militarism: Civilian and Military*, pp. 116–117, 118, 127–128. Revised edition © copyright 1959 by Meridian Books, Inc. © Copyright 1937 by W. W. Norton & Company, Inc. Reprinted by permission of The World Publishing Company.

ployed Bonaparte to save it from another revolution on the Left and a counterrevolution on the Right, it unwittingly rang its own death knell. After all, the new mass system had not entirely destroyed the old standing-army system; nor could it in the nature of things. It had necessarily relied upon the technical knowledge of the officers · and men who rose out of the standing-army system, and in the early phases of war and revolution another elite of officers had sprung up.

As things stood in April 1791, among these rising officers, Kellermann, their senior, was almost fifty-seven years old, Sérurier forty-nine, Berthier and Pérignon thirty-eight, Moncey thirty-seven, Lefèbvre and Masséna thirty-six, Augerau thirty-four, Jourdan thirty, Bernadotte and Brune twenty-nine, Bonaparte twenty-two, Marmont seventeen. On the enemy side, Wurmser was sixty-seven, Suvorov sixty-two, Brunswick fifty-seven, Blücher forty-nine, Wellington twenty-three. If we take the future twenty-five marshals of Napoleon, excluding the Pole Poniatowski, as prototypes of the new elite, most of them were not violent revolutionaries in a political sense — except three — and some, like Lefebvre, had been throughout the confusion men of order, protecting banking and other institutions from the plundering crowd.

Nor were they revolutionary soldiers in the sense that their military service started under the Revolution. Almost all of them were at least as well educated as Blücher. Six only of the future marshals belonged to the civilian class; the majority had been officers (nine) or soldiers (ten) in the time of the monarchy. All of the nine officers with one exception were nobles, though mostly of the lower ranks. Of the thirty-two general officers of the Armée d'Orient when it sailed for Egypt in 1798, sixteen had served as officers and eleven as non-officers in the army before 1789, and only five began their career as revolutionary soldiers. As is the case in every struggle for survival, there is no way to tell whether

the fittest for military performances had survived death by the guillotine or in the field. But good generals did survive those ordeals, carrying the war far beyond the frontiers of France. . . .

Among these officers, one was able to become master of all the soldiers and of the bourgeois state created by the Revolution: Napoleon Bonaparte. Much as historians have debated the secret of his achievement, no formula has been found to "explain" the "mystery." Nor is the cryptic word "genius" sufficient to account for it — "he seems to be above men," as a Paris paper wrote on his Italian successes. However, the stages of his climb are clear; winning command of the Army of Italy, he attacked the enemies at their feeblest points, which they proceeded to weaken for him yet further. With the glory of this campaigning he helped to destroy the civilian Directory and establish the Consulate and finally an Empire on its ruins. At home he defended the obvious property interests of the bourgeois and many gains of the Revolution, meantime making them pay dearly for the defense. In his enterprises abroad he exploited the manhood of France, enfranchised or not, in one war after another, waged for militaristic purposes: that is, not for the defense of France and the Revolution, but to realize his dreams of military power. Whether these dreams were the emanations of genius or the fantasies of a "conquering beast," he, the liquidator of the Revolution, wasted the assets which he had seized. Among his dissimulative and manipulative methods are many which illustrate the process by which the military way was transformed into a militaristic and Caesarian way. . . .

When Napoleon's military head was swollen into a militaristic head, the beginning of his end came in sight. "In war men are nothing, *one* man is everything," he wrote. His regard for men sank steadily as he advanced into the last phase, while his self-esteem, his inclination "to make images" out of touch with reality, grew and he was possessed by the *"rage des nombres."* The size of his armies outgrew his actual control, though he tried persistently to retain it by insisting on constant reports about the strength of the divisions. It is highly dubious whether he ever knew, or did not constantly overestimate, the exact number of men at his disposal on the day of battle. In such uncertainty he was inclined to convince himself by the sight of the masses of his troops; it gave him an intoxication from which the reports available on paper should have protected him. It was as if a merchant trusted for exact information the sight of his filled storehouse more than the written list of its contents.

The growing recklessness in the wasting of men and the rising distrust of the individual soldier, which none of the popular tricks of the *petit caporal* could hide, led to a tactical use of soldiers that was different from practice under the Republic, the Consulate, and the very first years of the Empire. This became particularly obvious in French attacks against an enemy in fortified positions. Instead of using, as before, *tirailleurs* in great bands, only companies of the light infantry in the regiments were deployed. For the main effect, reliance was placed on the moral shock of the close columns, advancing with drums beating. This tactical form was constantly employed in the Peninsular War. From beginning to end, none of the generals, Napoleon included, recognized that this was the main source of all the French disasters in Spain, whereas Wellington after Vimeiro (1808) acknowledged that such attack in column

against an infantry not previously shaken by the fire of infantry or artillery had as little chance as a cavalry attack against an intact infantry. So by his growing disregard for the lives of his men and by his resort to wasteful tactics, Napoleon wore out the human resources upon which he relied for his very predominance over France and Spain.

In the light of this record showing the transformation of Bonaparte, the soldier, into Napoleon, the militarist, some reasons for his downfall and the collapse of his system become apparent. As his egomania grew in size, he lost all sense of the proportions among things and of the limitations on human power, however great it may be at a given moment. The absence of this sense is a prime characteristic of militarism, and distinguishes it from the military way. In Napoleon's case it meant more than a loosening of his mental and physical grip on the material and human resources at his command. It meant a blind and stubborn incapacity to understand the imponderables in front of him. In the reckless use of mass armies for the attainment of his ambitions, he evoked from the bosom of half-slumbering feudal societies opposed to him the very force of mass armies and nationalism which smashed his system and sent him reeling into exile, where he tried, for the benefit of simpletons, to create a fiction of himself as the spirit of the Revolution incarnate — to cover his true significance as the spirit of militaristic counterrevolution incarnate.

IV. ENLIGHTENED DESPOT OR MODERN DICTATOR?

Philosopher Prince

GEOFFREY BRUUN

Geoffrey Bruun (1898–   ) is probably most widely known for his textbooks, including the much-used *A Survey of European Civilization*, which he wrote in collaboration with Wallace K. Ferguson and which has gone through several editions since its publication in 1936. Formerly Professor of History at New York University, he has since 1949 devoted himself almost exclusively to research and writing. His publications include biographies of Saint-Just and Clemenceau, a small volume on the enlightened despots, and *Europe and the French Imperium, 1799–1814*, to which this selection is the introduction.

O N DECEMBER 25, 1799, when Napoleon Bonaparte assumed his official duties as First Consul of the French Republic, the officer of the day reported to inquire the new password for the consular guard. *"Frédéric II,"* was the brief response, *"et Dugommier."* Observers curious to forecast the guiding principles of the new régime might have found something to ponder in this phrase, which linked the name of the great Frederick, most famous enlightened despot of the eighteenth century, with that of Dugommier, an obscure but valiant general of the French revolutionary armies. The spirit of enlightened autocracy, combined with the spirit of revolutionary zeal, were to be the twin arbiters of a new France. With the histrionic touch characteristic of him, General Bonaparte had coined the watchword, not of a day, but of an epoch.

The major misconception which has distorted the epic of Napoleon is the impression that his advent to power was essentially a dramatic reversal, which turned back the tide of democracy and diverted the predestined course of the revolutionary torrent. That this Corsican liberticide could destroy a republic and substitute an empire, seemingly at will, has been seized upon by posterity as the outstanding proof of his arrogant genius. To reduce his career to logical dimensions, to appreciate how largely it was a fulfillment rather than a miscarriage of the reform program, it is necessary to forget the eighteenth century as the seedtime of political democracy and remember it as the golden era of the princely despots, to recall how persistently the thinkers of that age concerned themselves with the idea of enlightened autocracy and how conscientiously they laid down the intellectual foundations of Cæsarism. Napoleon was, to a degree perhaps undreamed of in their philosophy, the son of the *philosophes*, and it is difficult to read far in the political writings of the time without feeling how clearly the century prefigured him, how in-

Pp. 1–5 "Prelude to Caesarism" from *Europe and the French Imperium, 1799–1814* by Geoffrey Bruun. Copyright 1938 by Harper and Row, Publishers, Incorporated. Reprinted by permission of the publisher.

eluctably in Vandal's phrase *l'idée a précédé l'homme.*

All the reforming despots of the eighteenth century pursued, behind a façade of humanitarian pretexts, the same basic program of administrative consolidation. The success achieved by Frederick the Great in raising the military prestige and stimulating the economic development of Prussia provided the most notable illustration of this policy, but the same ideals inspired the precipitate decrees of Joseph II in Austria, the cautious innovations of Charles III of Spain, the paper projects of Catherine the Great of Russia and the complex program pursued by Gustavus III in Sweden. Military preparedness and economic self-sufficiency were the cardinal principles guiding the royal reformers, but they also shared a common desire to substitute a unified system of law for the juristic chaos inherited from earlier centuries, to eliminate the resistance and confusion offered by guilds, corporations, provincial estates and relics of feudatory institutions, and to transform their inchoate possessions into centralized states dominated by despotic governments of unparalleled efficiency and vigor. In crowning the work of the Revolution by organizing a government of this type in France, Napoleon obeyed the most powerful political tradition of the age, a mandate more general, more widely endorsed, and more pressing than the demand for social equality or democratic institutions. Read in this light, the significance of his career is seen to lie, not in the ten years of revolutionary turmoil from which he sprang, but in the whole century which produced him. If Europe in the revolutionary age may be thought of as dominated by one nearly universal mood, that mood was an intense aspiration for order. The privileged and the unprivileged classes, philosophers, peasants, democrats, and despots all paid homage to this ideal. Napoleon lent his name to an epoch because he symbolized reason enthroned, because he was the philosopher-prince who gave to the dominant aspiration of the age its most typical, most resolute,

and most triumphant expression.

To the student accustomed to think of the eighteenth-century *philosophes* as heralds of the French Revolution, it must always prove a disappointment to realize how ambiguously they announced it. These knights of the pen, from Montesquieu to Turgot, whose criticism helped to dissolve the foundations of the old régime, were themselves no friends of revolution or of democracy. The ideal at which they aimed was a more rational order of society; but their remedy for the evils of despotism was, in general, more despotism, and their solution for the problems of an increasingly dynamic age was to make social institutions more stable and more static. A violent upheaval, factious assemblies, and mob rule had no part in their program, for they were more inclined to put their trust in the wisdom of princes than in the deliberations of parliaments. Because their agitation hastened a revolution which few of them foresaw and fewer would have applauded, they have been extravagantly honored by liberal historians. But these historians have not always felt it necessary to point out that the most logical fulfillment of the *philosophes'* ideals was not the republicanism of the Jacobin commonwealth, but the despotism of the First Empire.

The central clue to the reform program of the philosophers was their faith in natural law. Mankind, they agreed, stood on the threshold of a new and glorious era. All that was needed to unlock the millennium was a supreme legislator, a Euclid of the social sciences, who would discover and formulate the natural principles of social harmony. The mathematical generalizations which formed the ground plan of physics and astronomy had been propounded by a few bold thinkers, and it seemed a reasonable surmise that the fundamental laws of human society would likewise be discovered by some inspired genius rather than by a parliamentary assembly. This optimistic faith that a rational constitution for society might shortly be comprehended and codified was not confined to philosophical circles in France, it was the common property of almost all eighteenth-century thinkers. Even Immanuel Kant gave to the sanguine quest the imprimatur of his cautious approval as early as 1784 in his *Idea of a Universal History on a Cosmo-Political Plan*:

We will see if we can succeed in finding the cipher [to such a universal ground-plan for society] and then leave it to Nature to produce the man who can solve it. So, once, she brought forth a Kepler, who reduced the excentric orbits of the planets to an orderly formula in unexpected fashion, and a Newton who clarified the universal principles governing the natural order.

Once a legislator of outstanding genius had rationalized human institutions, it followed that each man would respect them because they would be in harmony with his reason and his instincts. In yielding obedience he would achieve complete liberty, for he would be responding to a categorical imperative, or, as Rousseau had expressed it, he would be identifying his individual volition with the general will. This concept of perfect liberty as the product of perfect laws was one of the finest flowers of eighteenth-century rationalism, but it is important to note that such laws could be introduced quite as easily by a despot as by a democratic assembly. The prayer attributed to Turgot in 1774, "Give me five years of despotism and France shall be free," expressed a hope which at the time few people considered paradoxical. The demand for liberty in the age of enlightenment did not necessarily imply a demand for popular government, however frequently later writers may have chosen to ignore the distinction.

A second possible misconception against which it is well to guard when considering the arguments of the *philosophes* concerns their use of the term *republic*. It is the modern habit to classify governments by their external form, but the political thinkers of the age of reason were interested in the functions of the ideal state rather than in its structure. A republic, to them, meant nothing much more specific than a well-governed commonwealth, and their use of such phrases as "republican monarchy" and "monarchical democracy" suggests the fluidity of their political terminology. "I give the name *Republic* to every state that is governed by laws," affirmed Rousseau, "no matter what its form of administration may be. . . ." The distinguishing characteristic of a republican society was then considered to be a certain health and good condition of the body politic, not the existence of any specific electoral machinery for assuring the primacy of the popular will. How such imprecision in the use of terms might facilitate the transition to a dictatorship is evident enough. Napoleon was able to insist, without inviting serious contradiction, that with the establishment of the consular régime "the Revolution was grounded upon the principles which had inspired it." Even the constitution of the Empire opened with the propitiatory phrase, "The government of the Republic is confided to an emperor," and the imperial coinage bore for several years the ambiguous superscription *République Française: Napoléon Empereur*.

The heritage of eighteenth-century philosophy thus aided in two respects the realization of Napoleon's projects for personal rule. By stressing the benefits which a genius on a throne might introduce, the political writers had popularized the idea of enlightened despotism. By leaving the ideal form of government undefined they made it possible for Napoleon to unite the republican and monarchical traditions in a workable formula of democratic despotism. It is easy, however, to overemphasize the ideological element in revolutionary politics. Fundamentally and practically Napoleon's popularity rested upon the fact that he rescued France from social demoralization and foreign threats. To the generation which welcomed his advent to power his régime represented the close of a dangerous experiment, a return to order and stability after a decade of perilous opportunism and incertitude.

Last Enlightened Despot

GEORGES LEFEBVRE

Georges Lefebvre (1874–1959) in the final decades of his life held a preeminent place among scholars of the French Revolution. He occupied the Chair of the History of the Revolution at the University of Paris and was the editor of the scholarly journal, the *Annales historiques de la Révolution française*. A prolific writer, he was the author both of pioneering monographs like *Les Paysans du Nord pendant la Révolution* (1924)—a new approach to revolutionary history—and *La Grande Peur* (1932), and works of synthesis such as his classic *Quatre-vingt-neuf* (1939), published in English as *The Coming of the French Revolution*, his survey, *La Révolution française* (1951), also published in English, and his *Napoléon* (1936). The last is not a biography, but a study of the Napoleonic Era in the European world. In it Lefebvre draws an acute and perceptive portrait of Napoleon, from which this selection is taken.

FOR A LONG TIME the republicans wanted to strengthen governmental authority, as the constitutions that they had given the vassal states demonstrated, not to mention the Cisalpine, fief of Bonaparte; in Holland the directors controlled the treasury; in Switzerland they appointed the functionaries; in Rome the judges as well; in these latter two republics the departments already had a "prefect." Unfortunately the Constitution of the Year III did not permit a revision before 1804. The coup d'état of 18 Fructidor had furnished an occasion that Sieyès, Talleyrand, and Bonaparte thought to exploit. It was allowed to escape; but in the Year VII they thought to provoke a new occasion. Without their realizing it the republicans were obeying a tendency, which ever since the civil war and the foreign war had begun, pushed the Revolution toward the establishment of a permanent omnipotent executive; that is, toward dictatorship. It was a social revolution and the dispossessed aristocracy did not confine itself to insurrection; with money from the enemy it exploited the de-

mands of the war, inexhaustible source of discontent, and notably the monetary and economic crisis, to turn the population against the government. The French did not want to go back to the *ancien régime*, but they were suffering, and they held their leaders responsible for it. At each election the counter-revolution hoped to seize power again. In 1793 the *Montagnards* had seen the peril and perpetuated the Convention until the peace. The Thermidorians had wished to restore the elective regime; immediately after, by the two-thirds decree, they had revived the Jacobin expedient. Then, the Directory, outflanked by the elections of the Year V, had returned to dictatorship, on 18 Fructidor. But while the constitution of the Year III remained in force, that dictatorship was threatened each year, required repeated use of force, and could not organize itself. There remained only to revive the principle of 1793 and to make its application permanent until peace, definitively reestablished, persuaded the counter-revolution to accept the new order. It is thus that the dictatorship of Napoleon

From Georges Lefebvre, *Napoléon* (Vol. XIV of *Peuples et civilisations, histoire générale*) (Paris: Presses universitaires de France, 3d edition, 1947), pp. 58–60, 63–66. Reprinted by permission of the Presses universitaires de France. [Editor's translation.]

is intimately bound to the history of the Revolution; whatever he may have said and done, neither he nor his adversaries were ever able to break that solidarity, and the European aristocracy perfectly understood it.

As in 1793, the Jacobins of the Year VII proposed to institute a democratic dictatorship, depending on the *sans-culottes* to prevail over the councils. Aided by the crisis that preceded the victory of Zurich, they had succeeded in wringing from the councils several revolutionary measures: the forced loan, the forbidding of conscripts to purchase replacements, the law of hostages, the annulling of delegations of public revenues that had been given to bankers and army contractors, the taxation of investments and salaries, the requisitions. They touched the bourgeoisie in their interests and forced them to take action; it is symbolic that the delegations of public revenues had been reestablished on the very evening of 19 Brumaire. The "idéologues" who gathered around Mme de Condorcet at Auteuil or in the salon of Mme de Staël did not want democratic dictatorship, nor even democracy. In some fragments of 1799, on the means "to terminate the Revolution" and on "the principles that ought to lay the foundations of the Revolution," Mme de Staël set forth their wish: to contrive a representative system that would assure power to the "notables" of wealth and talent. Being inspired by the decree of two-thirds, Sieyès, who had become a director, wished himself to appoint, with his friends, the new legislative bodies, which would be recruited thereafter by cooptation, the nation electing only the candidates. The men in office here saw, moreover, the advantage of perpetuating themselves in power.

To institute the dictatorship of the bourgeoisie, from the moment that the people were eliminated, there remained only the army. On the 18 Fructidor, Year V, the Directory had already had recourse to it, without the civil power, despite grave damage, having lost the controlling hand. The case this time was very different, because it was a matter of driving out undoubted republicans, not royalists. Only a popular general had a chance to win it over. The sudden return of Napoleon made him the choice. The wish of the nation that was invoked to justfiy the 18 Brumaire counted for nothing. It had welcomed Napoleon with joy because it knew him as a good general; but the Republic had conquered without him and the triumph of Masséna benefitted the Directory. The responsibility for the 18 Brumaire devolves on that part of the republican bourgeoisie that we call the *Brumariens* and, in whose first rank glitters Sieyès. They did not intend to abandon themselves to Bonaparte and had chosen him only as an instrument. Nevertheless, they had pushed him to power without posing any conditions, without even having traced out the essential lines of the new regime, and that is a proof of irremedial mediocrity. Bonaparte will not repudiate the "notables," because he, no more than they, was a democrat, and he needed them in order to govern. But on the evening of 19 Brumaire, when they had hastily organized the provisional Consulate, they were unable to persist in their illusions. The army had followed Napoleon and him alone. He was now the master. Whatever was said by him and his apologists, his power, by its origins, was a military dictatorship, now absolute. It was he who was going to resolve the questions on which depended the fate of France and of Europe. . . .

Under his soldier's habit, there were several men, and his fascinating attraction comes from that diversity as much as from the variety and the *éclat* of his gifts. He burned with the same appetites as the others, the Bonaparte of the Year III wandering without a sou in the midst of the *fête thermidorienne*, brushing the powerful of the day, the rich men and the pretty women. He always retained something of those days: a certain pleasure to subjugate those who had treated him contemptuously, a taste for ostentatious magnificence, the concern to gorge his family, the "clan," which had suffered from the same poverty, and also some memorable words of a bourgeois gentleman on the day of the coronation, "Joseph! if our father saw us!" He was no less animated and much earlier, by a more noble taste: that of knowing everything and understanding everything, a taste which, to be sure, served him greatly but which he first satisfied without underlying design.

As a young officer, he was an indefatigable reader and compiler, a writer, too, and one sees that if he had not attended Brienne, he could have become a man of letters. Entered in action, he remained a thinker; this man of war was never happier than in the silence of his study, amid his notes and his dossiers. The trait was attenuated; his thought became practical and he boasted of having repudiated "ideology"; he remained no less the man of the eighteenth century, rationalist and philosopher. Far from trusting himself to intuition, he counted on reason, on knowledge as a methodical effort. "I have the habit of foreseeing three or four months in advance what I ought to do, and I calculate on the worst; every operation ought to be made according to a system, because chance makes nothing succeed"; his insights he sees as the natural fruit of his patience. He is quite classic in his conception of the unitary state, constructed of a single piece following a simple and symmetrical plan. In rare instances, even intellectualism revealed itself in him by his sharpest trait: the dividing of his personality in two, the faculty of watching himself live and reflecting with melancholy on his destiny. From Cairo he had written to Joseph after having learned of the unfaithfulness of Josephine: "I have need of solitude and isolation. Grandeurs bore me, sentiment is withered; glory is stale. At twenty-nine years I have exhausted everything"; walking at Ermenonville, with Girardin, he will soon say: "The future will learn whether it would not have been better for the repose of the earth that neither Rousseau nor I had ever existed"; and when Roederer, visiting

with him the abandoned Tuileries, sighs, "General, this is sad," Bonaparte, first consul for two months, replies, "Yes, like grandeur." Thus, by a striking reverse, intellectualism comes to insinuate the romantic sadness of Chateaubriand and De Vigny in this firm and severe mind. But it is always only a flash, and he soon recovers.

Everything seems to push him into realistic politics and everything in its execution is realistic to the least detail. In the course of his rise, he made the rounds of human passions and learned to play upon them; he knew how to exploit interest, vanity, jealousy, and even dishonesty; he saw what one can get from men in exciting their sentiment of honor and in exalting their imagination; he is not unaware that one can subjugate them by terror. In the work of the Revolution he distinguished with a sure eye what was closest to the heart of the nation and that which was in accord with his despotism. To win over the French he presented himself at once as the man of peace and as the god of war. That is why it happens that he is ranked among the great realists of history.

He is that, however, only in execution. In him lives still another man, who has some traits of the hero and who must have been born when he was in military school, from his desire to dominate the world, where he felt himself scorned, and especially to equate himself with the half-legendary characters of Plutarch and of Corneille. What above all he is ambitious for is glory: "I live only in posterity; death is nothing, but to live vanquished and without glory, is to die every day." His eyes are on the masters of the world: Alexander, conqueror of the Orient, dreaming of the conquest of the world; Caesar, Augustus, Charlemagne, creators and restorers of the Roman Empire, whose names themselves imply the idea of the universal. It is not a matter there of a concrete notion that would serve as rule, as measure, and as limit to a political enterprise; they are examples that fire the imagination and give to action an inexpressible charm. He is impassioned less by the deeds of heroes than by the spiritual ardor of which they are evidence. Artist, poet of action, for whom France and humanity were only instruments, he expressed at Saint-Helena his sentiment of grandeur, when evoking the victory of Lodi and the awakening, in his conscience, of the will for power, he said magnificently, "I saw the world sink away below me as if I were carried off in the air." That is why it is vain to search for the goal that Napoleon assigned to his policy and the limit where he intended to stop; there was none. To partisans who were worried about this, he reported: "I reply always that I know nothing about it" or again, with profundity, despite the trivial form: "The place of God the father? Oh, I would not want it; it is a *cul-de-sac.*" Here we meet again in a psychological form, that dynamism of temperament, which strikes one at the first encounter. It is the romantic Napoleon, a force that is unleashed and for whom the world is only an occasion to act dangerously. But the realist is recognized not only by the ordering of means; he also determines his goal in taking account of the possible, and, if imagination and taste for grandeur can push him, he knows where he should stop himself.

Moreover, if Napoleon, as Molé well observed, escaped from that which is real, which his mind, on the other hand, was so capable of grasping, it was not only his nature that was responsible, but also his origins. When he arrived in France, he considered himself a foreigner and, until he had been expelled from Corsica by his compatriots, in 1791, he remained hostile to the French. To be sure, he sufficiently penetrated their civilization and their spirit to nationalize himself among them; if not, he never would have been able to become their chief; but he did not have time to incorporate himself into the French community and to take unto himself its national tradition to the point of considering its interests as the rule and the limit of his own action. He remained, himself, an uprooted man. Without class also; neither en-

tirely gentleman nor entirely of the people, he served the King and the Revolution without attaching himself to either the one or the other. That was one of the causes of his success, since he thus found himself perfectly at ease in raising himself above parties, and presenting himself as the restorer of national unity. But neither in the *ancien régime* nor in the new, did he draw upon principles that would have served him adequately as norms and limits. He was not restrained, like Richelieu, by dynastic loyalty that would have subordinated his will to the interests of his master, no more was he by a civic virtue that would have placed him at the service of the nation.

Upstart soldier, student of the philosophes, he detested feudalism, civil inequality, religious intolerance; seeing in enlightened despotism a reconciliation of authority and of political and social reform, he made himself its last and the most illustrious representative; in this sense he was the man of the Revolution. His passionate individualism, however, never accepted democracy, and he repudiated the great hope of the eighteenth century that gave life to revolutionary idealism: that of a humanity one day sufficiently civilized to be mistress of itself. Not even concern for his own security induced him to prudence like other men, because in the common sense of the expression he was disinterested, dreaming only of heroic and perilous grandeur. Moral restraint remained; but he was not in intellectual communion with other men in spiritual life; if he well knew their passions and turned them marvelously to his purposes, he retained only those that permit their enslavement, and he vilified all that raises them to sacrifice: religious faith, patriotic enthusiasm, love of liberty, because it seemed to him an obstacle. Not that he was impervious to these sentiments, at least in the time of his youth, because they turn easily into heroic action; but circumstances oriented him otherwise and walled him up within himself. In the splendid and terrible isolation of the will to power, restraint has no meaning.

The idéologues believed him one of theirs and did not suspect the romantic impulsion in him. The sole means perhaps of containing him would have been to keep him in a subordinate position in the service of a strong government. In pushing him to supreme power the *Brumariens* had lost their hold on him.

First Modern Dictator

ALFRED COBBAN

Alfred Cobban (1901–1968) was successively Reader in French History and Professor of French History at University College, University of London. His writing and teaching carried his influence far beyond the limits of his university, and he became one of the world's leading authorities on eighteenth- and nineteenth-century French history. His publications include a history of France since 1715 and many monographs, most of them concerning the French Revolution and its origins. In the 1960's he was in the eye of a scholarly storm over the interpretation of the French Revolution, a position he achieved by the publication in 1964 of his provocative *Social Interpretation of the French Revolution*. He was interested in political science as well as in history, and the combination of the two disciplines gave him a special qualification to judge the nature of Napoleon's rule in his book on dictatorship, from which this selection is taken.

O NE NEED not belittle Napoleon to hold that some form or other of dictatorship was, as Burke had prophesied, the inevitable outcome of the Revolution. The Republic, ruled after the fall of Robespierre by an increasingly narrow oligarchy of politicians, could not survive. Had the prisoner of the Temple, the little son of Marie Antoinette, lived, a monarchy might easily have been set up in his name. Had the brothers of Louis XVI shown any willingness to accept its basic social achievements, there might have been a Restoration at any time after 1795; but even moderate revolutionaries feared the return of a king tied to the *émigrés* and bent on revenge.

Although historians, wishing to draw a picture of Napoleon as the saviour of France, have exaggerated the defects of the Directory, at best it could not be regarded as a government likely to inspire popular enthusiasm. Too many of the politicians ruling France were corrupt, too many of their plans, both domestic and foreign, ended in disaster. The *jeunesse dorée* was parading the boulevards. Madame Récamier and Madame de Staël had stepped into the shoes of the great salonnières and were educating the revolutionary leaders in the ways of smart society. The bourgeois Puritanism of Robespierre had perished with him on the scaffold, sacrificed to the "triumphant nudities" of the future Madame Tallien, *notre dame de thermidor* and reigning deity of the Directory. The demimonde had been restored, if not the *monde*.

From Alfred Cobban, *Dictatorship: Its History and Theory* (New York: Charles Scribner's Sons, 1939), pp. 79–95. Reprinted by permission of Jonathan Cape, Ltd.

Indulgence was replacing terrorism as the order of the day, and revolutionary ardour was a thing of the past.

In central and local government, in the law, the Church, the land, foreign relations — in none of these fields had stability been achieved. Local administration was a chaos, the national elections a fraud, the currency worthless and the Treasury bankrupt. The government, living from hand to mouth, survived only with the aid of the loot sent home by its generals from conquered cities and provinces, though if the revolutionaries made war pay for itself they were certainly cleverer or luckier than most modern governments. Idealism was dead. War profiteers flaunted their riches, while the comrades of Robespierre and Saint-Just lurked in obscure hiding places or rotted in exile. The last futile flicker of Jacobinism died when the conspiracy of Babœuf was crushed, yet the country had no confidence in the groups of intriguers who had taken the place of the Jacobins — the Barras and Talliens, Reubells and Revellières. Only the army seemed a relatively stable point.

The emergence of the army as a leading factor in the political situation justified a fear which had possessed men as diverse as Robespierre and Burke. The armies of the *ancien régime* — small in size compared with the whole population, but possessing a monopoly of military power, attached by long service and tradition to the monarchy, officered by an hereditary aristocracy, and having in their *corps d'élite* an efficient and generally reliable force for use in any civil emergency — were a strong bulwark of the *status quo*. The Revolution could not have succeeded in France if the discipline of these troops had not cracked. Under the menace of foreign invasion the revolutionaries set about building up new armies by the system of universal compulsory military service. They were well aware that a small professional army was normally an instrument of the Crown and the nobles: a citizen army, it was thought, would be the defence of the people. Only a nation in arms, they believed, could be a free nation.

The belief that conscription naturally went with democracy has ever since been held on the continent, and it is indeed on the surface plausible enough. Further consideration might have been suggested by the fact that the system was first used by Frederick the Great, no great lover of liberty. To put the manhood of a nation through a course of military discipline, always to have in the ranks and under arms a large body of young men, forming a nation apart, officered necessarily by professional soldiers, and putting loyalty to its generals above any respect it might be supposed to have for civilian leaders, is a great source of strength to a state, but not necessarily to the Parliamentary form of government, especially if to this is added a smaller body of seasoned veterans, a potential praetorian guard for any would-be Emperor. Armies are not usually politically minded, the doings of parliaments do not interest them, loyalty is their strongest emotion, and if they look for anything in politics it is for a leader.

So it was with the French revolutionary armies. They had developed a passionate attachment to their more successful generals, and especially had fallen under the sway of the irresistible Bonaparte. Moreover, the professional interest had largely replaced the political, and their hostility could easily be aroused against the politicians who left them starved of supplies and pay. It must not be thought that the armies were anti-revolutionary in spirit. Among both men and officers probably more genuine republican patriotism lingered than in any other section of the French people. But they were easily capable of identifying republican government with the rule of a great general, so long as the name of king was not breathed and royalists were not openly brought back into favour. Thus, if one general had not led them to overthrow the civil government, another would. Napoleon saw this, and at the critical moment used his hold over the army to strike a decisive blow.

The first effective intervention of the

army in politics was in September 1797, when Augereau dispersed the Jacobin mob with the famous whiff of grape-shot: the echoes of his cannon were to sound through modern history. Two years later Bonaparte concerted his plans with a group of politicians, who, with the short-sighted astuteness of their kind, thought they could use him as their instrument. When he ordered his grenadiers to disperse the Five Hundred in 1799, the Revolution was over. The prestige of government, which had collapsed with the downfall of Bourbon divine right, could now, it was hoped, be rebuilt on the victories of French arms. The reign of reason had come to a premature end, and government in France was to venture on the fakir-like experiment of sitting on bayonets.

It must be granted that the support of the army was not enough by itself to set up and maintain a new government; but along with the army went military glory, conquest and the growing spirit of imperialist aggression. Not Brumaire but Marengo gave France to Napoleon. True, military conquest ran counter to the basic principles of the Revolution, but from the pacifism of the early Robespierre to the crusading fervour of the Brissotins, and from the struggle of Carnot and Reubell for "natural frontiers" to the imperialist wars of Napoleon, the transition was easy. Bonaparte himself had taken the decisive step in this process, when he forced the preliminaries of peace with Austria, signed at Leoben in April 1797, on the Directory, in spite of the opposition of Reubell. From the system of limited annexations and natural frontiers France now passed to a policy of imperialist expansion, from the possible to the impossible, and it was the ambition of Bonaparte that largely dictated the development.

French imperialism still wrapped itself in the tattered robes of revolutionary propaganda. Bonaparte was still to idealists like Revellière-lépeaux a "Mahomet of Liberty," in success the armed prophet of the new dispensation, in defeat the valiant defender of French independence. To the end the motive of defence was probably stronger in the French people than the lust of aggression, but that was not a fact of great political importance. It was later to be found almost a *sine qua non* of an imperialist war of self-defence. That a statement is ridiculous is no barrier to popular credence, as Napoleon rapidly discovered; for he was able to keep up the legend of the defence of France throughout his career. He returned from Elba in 1815, as he came back to France from Egypt in 1799, to save the country, and he went on saving it from conquest to conquest. Every battle was to be the final victory that would bring peace. France and Bonaparte were hardly to be expected to realize that only defeat could bring that to a power claiming the hegemony of Europe.

This search for peace was, it must be admitted, a necessary pretence, for when Bonaparte came to power after Brumaire it was above all because France believed that he could give her peace, internal and external. Among all the articles, manifestos, pamphlets, rhymes, music-hall sketches, which celebrated the *coup d'état,* says Vandal, there is not a single one in which is not to be found expressed the universal desire for peace, and to it Bonaparte responded, swearing in vibrant proclamations to bring back peace to France and Europe.

If the combination of military glory with the desire for peace formed the foundation of Bonaparte's authority, they were not the only elements contributing to it. France, which had not felt the hand of a master since the fall of the great Committee of Public Safety, urgently wanted a government. The demand was not yet for a leader, a chief of the state. Nowhere does one find the cry, says Vandal, "A man, we need a man." Modern Caesarism, he adds, is a legacy of Bonaparte. One would be tempted to modify his statement. In the situation in which France found herself the demand for a leader, a saviour of society, was almost inevitable. That this desire was not consciously formulated is doubtless true; it was hardly to be expected that it should be, for it was the first time that such a situation had appeared in modern history. But after ten years of revolution uncertainty had lasted too long: authoritarian government was needed to end the strain, and to restore a feeling of stability. This was the real meaning behind the meaningless maxim of Sieyès — 'Authority must come from above and confidence must come from below.' Although the internecine struggles of the earlier revolutionary period had died down, their memory was fresh, and the fear remained that they might at any time break out again.

Bonaparte came to power because his name provided a new source of authority, but at the same time the principle of the sovereignty of the people had established too firm a hold over men's minds to be abandoned. Some means of reconciling this principle with the rule of one man had to be found. Emotionally this was easy: the sovereignty of the people had become fused with nationalism, and Napoleon through his victories had come to be a living symbol of the national greatness. But to add the appearance of free choice he adopted the method used by the Jacobins in presenting their Constitution of 1793 to the country — the plebiscite. Sieyès and the men of Brumaire had themselves presented this device to Bonaparte, when they incorporated in the Constitution of the year VIII the name of the First Consul, Citizen Bonaparte; so that when it was submitted to the popular vote, it was as much a plebiscite on Bonaparte as a vote for a constitution. The votes on the life consulate in 1802 and on the establishment of the Empire in 1804 are mere sequels. By these popular votes democracy, or at least the principle that all authority is derived from the people, was to be triumphantly vindicated by the election of Napoleon to the post of supreme power in the state. In this way arose, in the modern world, the idea that one man might himself represent the will of the people, and be invested with all the authority of the most despotic ruler in the name of democracy. The idea of sovereignty, freed from all restraints, and transferred to the people, had at last given birth to the first modern dictatorship.

The Jacobin attempt at dictatorship from the left had failed. Napoleon came to power as a dictator from the right — not, of course, as a leader of the old reactionary party, but as a dictator supported by the propertied classes, the financiers and commercial men, the upper bourgeoisie, and speculators, who had made large fortunes out of the revolution and had bought up church or crown lands or the property of *émigrés*, with worthless *assignats*. The financial blunders and economic incompetence of the revolutionaries had at least allowed these men to make large fortunes; but as a final bankruptcy loomed nearer and nearer, the Directory was driven to ever more desperate expedients. It even proposed to suspend the assignments on the taxes allocated to the government contractors, to deprive them of the right of collecting payment themselves, and to introduce a progressive tax. The contractors and speculators, in the words of Vandal, threw themselves into the arms of Bonaparte to defend them from this blow. He returned from Egypt penniless, to face the mounting debts of Josephine; a group of bankers formed a syndicate to come to his aid, and they provided the financial resources without which the *coup d'état* of Brumaire would have been impossible. Direct benefits to its financial backers followed, for the measures proposed against the contractors were dropped at once, and ten days later the progressive tax was abolished.

While Bonaparte needed the solid advantages that the support of the financiers and bankers could give, he also had to preserve the confidence of the masses. Military glory and the hope of peace went a long way towards this, but economic benefits were also required. The peasantry was fairly easily contented: the reassertion of law and order and therefore the revival of prosperity, a conservative social policy, a gradual return to Catholicism, along with a guarantee that the alienated lands and feudal dues of the Church and the *noblesse* would never be returned — and the peasantry were satisfied. The populace in the towns required more management. For this reason Bonaparte's relations with the monied men were a carefully guarded secret. Indeed, in public he declared himself the enemy of the financiers and the government contractors, and after he had become First Consul he did not hesitate to fling one of them to the wolves as evidence of his own high principles; though when the arrest and examination of this scapegoat for a whole class had received sufficient publicity, he was secretly rescued, at a price. This reputation as an enemy of the speculators was an important element in the popularity which Bonaparte was winning in the poorer quarters of Paris. From General to Consul and from Consul to Emperor, he managed to keep the devotion of the Parisian working-classes: they loved and admired him, says Aulard, far more than they had ever admired and loved Robespierre or Marat.

Bonaparte's genius lay in his capacity for combining with this popular adulation a conservative and authoritarian system of government. France as a whole demanded a government which would guarantee the country against a revival of terrorism without handing it back to the *ancien régime*. The fear of a Jacobin revival was still strong in France and it was a force which Bonaparte used to the fullest degree. It played the part which fear of Communism has played in modern Germany. With its aid he took the critical step of ordering the Grenadiers to disperse the legislative body. At the very root of his authority was the magnificent, incredible lie of the dagger attack upon him by Jacobins in the meeting of the Five Hundred. Incredible as it might be, the country believed it.

It is not true to say that Bonaparte rescued France from the rule of the extreme revolutionaries, for the Directory had already suppressed the Jacobins and the mob of Paris, and the First Consul merely inherited their success. But he certainly carried on, and even exaggerated the trend to the right, welcoming in particular any moderates or even royalists who would accept his authority. Although he won over more than a few of the leading Jacobins and incorporated them in his bureaucracy, to those who would not sacrifice their principles he remained implacably hostile. The royalists who, in December 1800, attempted to blow up Napoleon when he was driving to the Opera, were never discovered; but their conspiracy was used by the First Consul, not as a reason for taking action against the many known royalists, but as a pretext for police measures against the republicans, ending in the exile to the Seychelles or French Guiana of nearly one hundred Jacobins, well over half of whom perished. The murder of the duc d'Enghien in 1804 was merely a warning to the royal family that Napoleon would stop at nothing in the defence of his regime. A carefully calculated act of terrorism against the Bourbons, it did not imply any hostility to royalists who were ready to abandon their king.

As well as ex-royalists, Bonaparte summoned the clericals to his banner. He made the most energetic efforts to win over the Church, suppressed anti-ecclesiastical societies, such as the Theo-philanthropes, withdrew the support of the government from the Constitutional Church, and as soon as he dared bought the alliance of Rome by the Concordat; subsequently, when it was too late for the Church to withdraw, passing the Ordinances, which achieved what the kings of France had struggled to gain for centuries, and made the Church in France for all effective purposes a department of the state. The Pope thought he had won a powerful supporter, but found that he had merely submitted to a master.

Taking into account all these diverse sources of support, it is comparatively easy to understand how Napoleon was able to make himself the leader of France. But if it was to be permanent his power had to have a more concrete basis. A political system capable of sustaining his authority had to be erected. This meant, first, the creation of a governmental machine dependent on his will alone, and then the occupation of all the key positions in the state by an army of personal supporters. Here, the centralizing trend, which had struggled with the elective principle throughout the Revolution, finally triumphed in the creation of the prefectoral system with its hierarchy of officials. In the Napoleonic bureaucracy revolutionary sentiments received their due with the application of the principle of equality, interpreted as *la carrière ouverte aux talents*. Ten years of revolutionary turmoil had thrown up plenty of talent from all ranks of French society, and Napoleon had no difficulty in filling his administration and officering his army with men of ability, and men who, owing everything to him, would be his devoted followers.

Supported thus by a powerful political machine, his rule sanctioned by the will of the people, his person idolized by the army, trusted by the men of property and the peasants, and backed by the Church, Napoleon was in a position to gather the whole of France into his hand. Terrorism he used comparatively little as an instrument of government: it was hardly necessary. Marat, Robespierre and the Directory had already removed most of those who were not amenable to influence. Moreover it is only fair to credit Napoleon with an appreciation of the fact that terrorist methods are a sign of weakness rather than of strength.

Although he had risen to power by the Army, Napoleon never made the mistake of over-estimating the power of force in governing a country or of under-estimating the power of opinion, as hosts of typically Napoleonic *obiter dicta* bear witness. All the factors capable of influencing public opinion were mobilized for the maintenance of his regime — the Church inculcated obedience; the Press suffered a rigid censorship and its news was dispensed through official journals; the stage and the arts were set to the task of glorifying the Emperor; literature, rather unwillingly, was to be harnessed to his chariot; education

was organized, with *lycées* and one central university, to enforce discipline in the academic world; finally, Napoleon's dispatches, comparable indeed with Caesar's, were a series of masterpieces of propaganda. The *ancien régime*, because it had neglected the people, had seldom condescended to tell them lies. Napoleon "erected mendacity on a hitherto unparalleled scale into an art of Empire."

We have been attempting to analyse the real reasons why Napoleon was able to gain and keep power, but though these would have been effective by themselves, it must not be supposed that he did not perform any services to France other than the rather doubtful one of winning battles and extending his sway over the greater part of Europe. The codification of the laws, even though this was only the completion of years of work by the revolutionary lawyers — the establishment of a sound financial system, presided over by the new Bank of France — the restoration of stability to land ownership, the economic activity of the *préfets*, devoted to building up the prosperity of their *départements* — all these and much more must go on the credit side of the balance. Mostly, it is true, they represent the work of the First Consul. As Emperor Napoleon took far more than he gave to France, and in the end the sum total perhaps hardly represents a great return for fifteen years of despotic rule.

More important than what Napoleon did was what he was. Of his colossal executive capacity and power of decision there can be no question. Lacking the higher forms of creative genius, he was still intellectually the superior of all his experts. It was not this side of his personality, however, which was most valuable to him as a leader of men. His intellect would never have made him an emperor without his appeal to the non-intellectual elements which are the driving forces in men and nations, — his capacity for catching and communicating emotion, his handsome appearance in youth, his charm of manner, his eloquence, and his knack of coining effective phrases.

His life was a series of dramatic gestures and he was his own press agent. From the beginning of his career — take, for instance, the words with which he was supposed to have stopped a Marseillais about to butcher one of his victims — "Man of the South, let us save this unfortunate" — to the end, when defeated and flying, he could still turn an elegant phrase, "I come, like Themistocles, to seat myself at the hearth of the British people" — his career is punctuated with memorable, if sometimes apocryphal, sayings.

Wellington and Castlereagh remained unmoved even at the last of these, but the theatrical disposition, the proneness to picturesque attitudes of the Corsican, was well fitted to catch the fancy of a Romantic generation, to win the admiration of the youthful Goethe, to inspire a Beethoven, or to make him the idol of a Byron, even if the melodramatic scenes which comprise his career are only the pseudo-heroics of an Ossianic hero. This association between Napoleon and the great Romantics is no mere accident: it deserves to be emphasized, because it establishes a connection at the beginning of the nineteenth century between Romantic ideas and dictatorship, which will emerge with greater effect when we come to study the origins of contemporary dictatorship.

Napoleon appealed to the Romantic imagination in part because he was a supreme individualist, a complete representative of the emancipation of the ego. If ordinary moral laws did not exist for him, that was one of his principal sources of strength. The politician who is completely emancipated from moral prejudices will naturally have an advantage over those who are liable to have their freedom of action occasionally hindered by moral considerations; whilst the people will admire a ruler in whom the absence of inhibitions gives them vicarious pleasure. Only an adventurer could have risen to fame as Napoleon did, and he remained an adventurer until the day when the *Bellerophon* carried him to an island where there was no room for more adventures. His very wars were a brigand's campaigns for loot, and diamonds, it is said, were found sewn in the upholstery of his carriage after Waterloo. He always cheated at cards. He was a worthy peer of the Renaissance Italian tyrants and the twentieth-century dictators.

Napoleon was the architect of his own greatness, and his ability alone held him on his throne. He knew it himself. "My position," he said, "is entirely different from that of the old sovereigns. They can live a life of indolence in their castles. . . . Nobody contests their legitimacy, nobody thinks of replacing them. . . . Everything is different in my case. . . . Within and without my dominion is founded on fear. If I abandoned the system I should be immediately dethroned." A regime cannot escape from its origins: and here at least Napoleon frankly recognized that war was a necessity for him. He had come bearing pledges of peace, but that was precisely what he could never give France. War made him necessary to France, and at the same time created the psychological atmosphere in which the continuance of his rule was possible. It is arguable, of course, that the practically continuous war while Napoleon ruled France was the result of the hostility of Europe, but whichever way one looks at it, the association between Napoleon's dictatorial system of government and his continual wars is certainly no mere coincidence.

What Napoleon had won by the sword it seemed he would have to keep by the sword. Gradually he became aware that if his power was to endure and to be handed on to a successor it would have to be put on a different basis. Dictatorship, aping the *ancien régime,* would have been more than a little ridiculous, were it not for the power that Napoleon represented. All the panoply of Empire which Napoleon created, his court, with its ancient pomp and ceremony, and its new Napoleonic nobility, was directed to one end: it was an attempt to wrap his new absolutism in the old mantle of divine right, and to legitimatize himself in the eyes of Europe. Hence his increasing reliance on former royalists. They alone knew how to obey, he said. Hence too his marriage with the Austrian Archduchess. All was in vain. Not that there was yet any fear of revolution. The army remained loyal, and the Prefects held the country firmly in their grasp. Enthusiasm had waned, but there was little sign of active opposition inside France. Foreign armies were needed to overthrow the Napoleonic system.

The country as a whole seems to have accepted with extraordinary passivity his fall, the return of the Bourbons, the Hundred Days and the final defeat. Political life in France, so hectic for a few years after 1789, was dead. During the brief interlude in Paris between Elba and Waterloo Napoleon tacitly admitted the failure of his dictatorship, and attempted by re-erecting his power on constitutional bases to connect it again with its revolutionary origins. In vain: the Napoleonic essay in constitutional monarchy never had time to come to life, nor is there any evidence that it could ever have lived. The greatest dictator in modern history fell, as he had risen, by war, and dragged out his remaining years in the midst of petty squabbles on a miserable tropical island. Meanwhile Europe set about reconstituting the reign of divine right, or putting Humpty Dumpty together again.

Precursor

FREDERICK B. ARTZ

Frederick B. Artz (1894–   ) is one of the few undergraduate teachers of history in America who have had *Festschrifts* published in their honor. A *Festschrift for Frederick B. Artz* appeared in 1964 near the close of Artz's more than forty years of teaching European history at Oberlin College. In those years he has also been active in research and writing. The titles of his well-known books—*The Mind of the Middle Ages; Reaction and Revolution, 1814–1832; From the Renaissance to Romanticism: Trends in Style in Art, Literature, and Music, 1300–1830; France under the Bourbon Restoration*—indicate the wide range of his interests and suggest his gift for synthesis and generalization, a gift that he utilized, at the height of Adolph Hitler's power, in making a comparison of the two Napoleons and the fascist dictators of the twentieth century.

H AVING SEEN the rise of the first and third Napoleons, let us examine their regimes after they attained power. Both came in on a program of peace abroad and of reconstruction and the appeasement of all factions at home. Both dictators soon showed themselves "crowned Benthams." Napoleon I made peace with the church, reorganized the public finances, cleaned up the administrative system, codified the law, and set in operation a national system of education. All were projects of earlier revolutionary regimes; he pushed them ahead, put his capital N on them all and claimed

From Frederick B. Artz, "Bonapartism and Dictatorship," *South Atlantic Quarterly*, XXXIX (1940), 40–45, 48–49. Reprinted by permission of the Duke University Press.

the credit. Much of the credit Napoleon deserved. His law codes, his national bank, his system of state education, his local administration, and even his Legion of Honor are still alive. His success lay in the fact that he was a tireless worker, with a superhuman capacity for combining minute technical knowledge with a sweeping imaginative grasp. "None," says Fisher, "could tear his secret from the specialist with such dexterity." He took his aides where he could find them; among his marshals were the sons of a wine merchant, a barrel maker, a miller, a tax collector, an innkeeper, and a mason. Among his prefects were nobles of the old regime, Girondists, and Jacobins, free-thinkers, Calvinists, and Catholic Ultramontanes. For every talent he tried to find a use, provided that each would submit to his will. He was everywhere the reformer, the social geometer, "one of these rare men," continues Fisher, "who assume that everything they come across from a government to a saucepan, . . . is capable of amendment. . . . When he visited a town, he would throw out plans for avenues and parks, clarify the municipal finance, consolidate the charitable endowments, cross-question the traders and manufacturers . . . and leave the whole place thrilling with new ideas and the bustle of change." His desire was always to obtain quick results; about the distant consequence he was indifferent and blind. The energies of the French people and of the peoples conquered before 1810 were released, intensified and coordinated, and the first decade of Napoleon's rule, following on the confusion of the Directory, seemed to be all the dreams of the benevolent despots come true. "Napoleon," said Goethe of this phase of the Emperor, "was the expression of all that was reasonable, legitimate and European in the revolutionary movement."

Napoleon III (1851–1870) tried to imitate all this. In his manifesto of 1852 he declared: "Certain people say the Empire is war. I say the Empire is peace. . . . I confess however that I, like the Emperor have many conquests to make. I wish, like him, to . . . reconcile dissident parties, to turn back again into the stream of the great popular river those hostile side currents which . . . lose themselves without profit to anyone. I wish to conquer for religion, for morality, and for prosperity that part of the population, still so numerous, which in . . . a country of faith . . . scarcely knows the precept of Christ . . . , which in the heart of the most fertile country . . . can scarcely enjoy the prime necessities. . . . We have immense districts . . . to clear, roads to open, harbors to dig, . . . our network of railways to complete. . . . Such are the conquests that I meditate, and all of you . . . are my soldiers."

These proved to be no vain words. Napoleon III gave the working class some improved housing, co-operative banks and stores, some old age and accident insurance, and finally the right to form trade unions and to strike. He had roads and canals improved, large areas drained and brought under cultivation; the railroads increased six-fold, and the steam force utilized by industry more than quintupled. Hausmann rebuilt Paris. Most of the provincial cities were extensively overhauled. Napoleon III, like his uncle, tried to regulate the economic life of his state; the regulations of the Second Empire show some regard for the working man, though with both Napoleons the advantage was always on the side of capital.

These wholesale ameliorations characterized both the First and the Second Empires, though it should never be forgotten that Napoleon III created nothing comparable to the Codes, the Concordat, the Université de France, the Bank of France or the administrative system of the First Napoleon. Both emperors were, in some degree, trying to distract men from the loss of their liberties; as Hulner said of the Second Empire, the two Napoleons were both "progressive and repressive." Both regimes, though they were despotic, made concessions to the spirit of the time and set up fake parliamentary institutions. These lath-

and-plaster assemblies, one of which could debate bills without voting and another which might vote without debating, gave to the regimes the appearance of democratic virtues while the tyrant enjoyed the solid satisfactions of dictatorship. The real work of governing was in the hands of the Council of State — on which Mussolini's Grand Council is modeled — and the prefects. The Council of State was a body of men eminent in technical knowledge, who transacted a huge amount of business in secret. A selected group of young men destined for the administration were allowed to attend the sessions. Next to the Emperor this council was the central motive force of the whole machine, but the Emperor's constant attention was necessary. So completely did both the First and Second Empires depend upon the will of the dictator that had either emperor been seriously ill for a month the whole Empire would have sickened.

Decisions were carried out by the prefects scattered through the departments; they executed the emperor's will, guided opinion, manipulated elections, watched the schools, the priests and the press. Behind everything stood the army. Grave questions were referred to a popular plebiscite which was based on the idea back of Sieyès' maxim: "Confidence from below, authority from above." Both emperors made much of the popular mandates for their dictatorships. The people were supreme though they had left all decisions to the leader who knew their needs better than they did themselves. "My policy," said Napoleon I, "consists in governing men as the greatest number wish to be governed. That, I think, is the way to recognize the sovereignty of the people." Napoleon III insisted that the "nature of democracy is to personify itself." It was a wonderful scheme for giving the masses the illusion that they were masters of their masters. In spite of pressure and manipulation of elections, both Napoleons had, until their downfall in war, the support of the overwhelming majority of the French peasants.

This meant the majority of the nation. There can be no doubt of that, though it must always be borne in mind that the choice was only between the man in power or chaos. And as in the Fascist and Nazi regimes, there was no representation nor protection of political minorities.

The church and the school were both forced under state control. Believing that a religious people is easier to govern, and at the same time wishing to separate the church from the old royalist cause, both Napoleons favored the priests as a "sacred gendarmerie." The Catholic Church got sick of the arrangement and proved to be more than either Bonaparte could handle; long before 1815 and 1870 the clergy paid only lip service to the regime. The schools were more successfully regimented. The dominant note for both empires is shown in a statement of Napoleon I: "There will never be a fixed political state of things in this country until we have a body of teachers instructed on established principles. So long as the people are not taught from their earliest years whether they ought to be republicans or royalists, Christians or infidels, the state cannot properly be called a nation."

The press was muzzled and public meetings forbidden; the secret police of both Napoleons were the most efficient Europe ever knew before the twentieth century. State prisons were established, as Napoleon I said for "all who could neither be brought to trial nor set at liberty without endangering the security of the state." In 1814 there were 2,500 political prisoners in French jails; in 1851 over 26,000 were thrown into prison, though by 1853, after 2,000 had been sent to Cayenne and some 8,000 to 10,000 shipped to Algeria, the government could say that there were few political prisoners in France. The censorship from 1799 to 1814 and again from 1851 to 1867 was the most severe Western Europe had known since the first decades of the Counter-Reformation. The pattern had been set by the highly republican Convention of 1793 to 1795, but Napoleon I improved on his model. The press was not only censored — under the Second Empire the government appointed the editors of the opposition papers, certainly a delightful anomaly — but the press was also widely used for elaborate propaganda favorable to the regimes. Both Napoleon I and Napoleon III, like Hitler and Mussolini, preached liberty to all oppressed nationalities abroad while maintaining a stern repression at home.

Literature languished; Mme. de Staël, the only independent French spirit under the First Empire, had to live in exile. "There is a complaint that we have no literature," said Napoleon I, "it is the fault of the minister of the interior." Exile was the lot of Hugo and Quinet under the Second Empire. Those who stayed like Chateaubriand under Napoleon I and Baudelaire, Flaubert, Leconte de Lisle, the Goncourts, Zola, Saint-Beuve, Renan, Thiers, and Michelet under Napoleon III, either buried themselves in scholarship or cynically sought the ivory tower of art.

When Napoleon returned from Elba in 1815, he had granted France a liberal constitution, the "Acte Additionnel." This deathbed gesture of the first Napoleon had been made a cardinal feature in the apocalyptic campaign of Saint Helena and had formed a sort of Paradise Regained theme in the pamphleteering of Louis Napoleon. So after the Italian War of 1859, when the old appeals were failing, Napoleon III, the perfect adventurer, drew a new arrow from his quiver, "L'Empire Libéral." Actually the liberalizing of the regime between 1860 and 1870 was undertaken in order to rally support for the failing forces of the Second Empire. One lot of dictatorial ballast after another was thrown out; in 1860 the deputies were granted the right of drawing up an answer to the emperor's annual address; a year later they were allowed to vote the budget by sections. In 1867 the deputies were permitted to question the ministers, and the censorship of the press was relaxed. Finally, in 1869 and 1870 the Legislative Body was allowed to initiate laws and the

ministry was made responsible to parliamentary control. But four months after Napoleon III said, "the edifice has been crowned with liberty . . . more than ever before we look forward to the future without fear," the Second Empire itself had collapsed at Sedan. It would probably not have lasted anyway; its mistakes and its humiliations were too numerous, its secret police had alienated the workers, the concessions to parliamentarianism were made too late, and the regime of Napoleon III had lived too long in sin ever to become respectable. Moreover, no real collaboration would have been possible between men who loathed liberty and men who detested the Empire.

The analogies between the Bonapartist regimes and the Fascist dictatorships are obvious. All arose out of political and social crises in which the various groups that wanted "order" rallied to the dictator. The support of these regimes lies in the fears of the peasants and the middle classes. All came into power because the older controlling forces became divided and seemed unable to meet the needs of troublous times, while, during the same period, the radical opposition was unable to swing the masses over to their side. All elaborate mythologies of why and how they rose and for what they stand. All hate intellectuals, all appeal to practical men who want quick and showy results, all promise all things to all men, all make use of a sense of tarnished national glory, all use wars and war scares to keep themselves in power, all like to talk about their love of peace. All perfect the secret police and the censorship; all use the schools and the press for propaganda; all are backed by the army; all are sanctioned by the ritual of the plebiscite. All perish in war.

The essential differences, however, are less evident. There are, first, the contrasts due to the changes in economic and social organization; parallels or contrasts involving the opening of the nineteenth century, the middle of that century and the second and third decades of the twentieth can never be very accurate. Some contrasts, however, stand out. Neither Napoleon nor his followers were such nobodies as were Mussolini and the Fascists before 1922 and Hitler and the Nazis before 1933; the present Fascist dictatorships are much more than the Bonapartist regimes an affair of the lower middle class. Both Napoleons came in on a peace program; Mussolini and Hitler enter history rattling the sabre. The two Napoleons worked with the Catholic Church and used it; the totalitarian objectives of Mussolini and Hitler have brought them into an insoluble conflict with the Church. Neither Napoleon was obsessed with a desire to wipe out the class struggle; neither had an organic theory of the state; both the First and Second Empires rose and fell without benefit of Hegel or Marx. Both Napoleons, at stages of their careers, considered their regimes as transitional to a democratic order; in that sense, both were dictators in the Roman tradition. Any attempts to democratize the present Fascist regimes after the manner of Napoleon III would pitch them into civil war. Neither Napoleon leaned on an organized party or had a private army; both leaned on the real army. Neither Napoleon was hysterical or brutal, neither had racial theories, and finally, neither ever exhorted millions through a microphone.

CONCLUSION

What, then, are we to think of Napoleon? There can be no single answer now in this, the Emperor's third century as, the reader has seen in the preceding selections, there was none among historians writing in his first and second centuries. Judgments in the 1970's, like those of all the preceeding decades, will vary with the values, the political convictions, and the views of human motives in the minds of the beholders. Yet among contemporary professional historians, separated by time and distance from the passions and quarrels of the Revolution and the succeeding century and trained in the dispassionate judgment of evidence, one can find an area of considerable agreement on Napoleon's abilities, his accomplishments, and his influence. The reader of this book may legitimately ask, how would one of these historians answer the four big questions posed in the book?

Was Napoleon the defender of the Revolution or its destroyer? The answer must now be that he was in some degree both. The Revolutionary heritage in 1799, when he assumed power as First Consul, was varied, and parts of it were contradictory with other parts. Some, such as the elimination of feudal dues, equality before the law, legally free choice of careers, were irreversible, but among other elements of the heritage, Napoleon could chose what he would preserve and consolidate. In choosing he necessarily rejected some elements (for example the Convention's projected social security system, its conception of education as a public service, and the limited redistribution of property). In some areas he drew less on the Revolution than directly on the Enlightened Despots (for example, in his religious policy) or on the early Bourbons (for example, in his administrative organization of the country under prefects, successors of Louis XIII's intendants). In short, he both accepted and rejected the Revolution, as he did the old Regime, using what served his purposes and goals, discarding the rest.

Was Napoleon the guardian of France's natural frontiers or an aggressor and expansionist? When he seized power in 1799, he took over a France whose frontiers had been extended by the conquests of the Revolutionary armies to the Rhine and the Alps. He avowed that he then wanted only the end of the long years of war but that France's enemies would accept peace only under coercion. Renewing the war, he defeated Austria in northern Italy and southern Germany and forced the Hapsburgs to make peace and to recognize France's territorial gains. England, stripped of allies, agreed to a peace in 1802. Then, Napoleon declared, the Revolution and its wars were finally ended. But his peace lasted little more than a year. Again, he insisted, war was forced upon him by envious and fearful European monarchs, and he was obliged to defend France and the Revolution. But war was his deliberate choice. Had he refrained from interference in the affairs of France's neighbors, opened French markets to English trade, and avoided the appearance of preparing to reestablish the colonial empire, peace could well have been preserved. But he was a soldier, accustomed to the use of arms to resolve problems. He had at his disposal a large, experienced, well-trained army, commanded by able, young officers anxious for further employment, honors, and riches, and they were a potential source of political trouble at home if left in the doldrums of peace. Beginning in 1805 Napoleon's armies were for eight years fighting far beyond France's frontiers. Not until late 1813 and 1814 were they truly defending those frontiers and then against attack that Napoleon's aggression had invited.

Was Napoleon a military genius or only the one of several able generals born of the Revolutionary wars who happened to avoid death or eclipse in military or political battles? Some of his operations bear the mark of genius — the First Italian Campaign, Ulm, Austerlitz — but against them one must place the disastrous intervention in Spain and the catastrophic invasion of Russia, and if one lists the major victories and the major defeats, one will find the latter list the longer. Napoleon inherited from his predecessors of the 1790's, an army far superior to those of his enemies. It was a mass army of free citizens, stirred by an ideal as well as by the usual, less-exalted motives, and led by officers risen by ability. His opponents in the early years fought with old style professional armies conscripted from the lowest strata of society, held together by brutal discipline, and commanded by aristocratic officers. Napoleon knew how to use his superior army effectively, and as long as he had it and his opponents had lesser forces, he won conspicuous victories. But he wasted and lost his great army in the endless fighting in Spain, and he could never re-create it. In his later years he fought with an army diluted by thousands of foreign conscripts and by increasingly disillusioned and reluctant French draftees, and commanded by generals growing tired and cautious. On the other side of the battle lines the enemy armies were improving in both command and morale. Without his superior army Napoleon after 1809 had a military record that lacks the signs of genius. We can ask, might not any of several Revolutionary generals have done as well as he had they achieved command of the French army in 1799?

Is Napoleon to be understood better as the last of the Enlightened Despots or as the first of the modern dictators? Similarities between Napoleon and the fascist dictators — Adolf Hitler and Benito Mussolini — can be found. Like them he defended established interests while posing as a revolutionary, won mass support while dismantling the institutions of democratic government, cared little for individual liberties, exploited the ambitious nationalism of his subjects, and distracted domestic opposition by engaging in foreign adventures. But to equate Napoleon with the twentieth-century dictators is anachronistic. He was a child of the eighteenth-century, moved by the rationalist ideas of the Enlightenment, not a product of the dislocations of nineteenth- and twentieth-century industrialization, urbanization, and disillusion. Enlightened Despotism was part of his personal experience; Frederick

the Great of Prussia, Joseph II of Austria, Louis XVI's reforming ministers were contemporaries of his early years. He had also witnessed the Revolutionary assemblies' attempts to apply the same Enlightened ideas by democratic and parliamentary means and observed their failures. Once securely in power, he returned to the despotic methods of the Fredericks and the Josephs, and his domestic goals were comparable to theirs.

The judgments offered in this conclusion reflect the tendency of recent scholarly writing to reduce Napoleon to mortal size. A distinguished English historian of France a few years back called Napoleon's regime "a temporary expedient" and concluded that there is "nothing truly remarkable about his achievements." An influential French school of historians, the *Annalistes* mentioned in the "Introduction" of this book, minimizes the role of great men in history, even Napoleon. "Let us not deceive ourselves," wrote one of them in the 1970's. "From 1800 to 1815 France changed very little." Napoleon's activities were on "the frothy surface" of history. He did not influence the movement or distribution of population; his policies neither significantly speeded nor significantly slowed French industrialization nor notably altered agricultural production. After his rule, as before it, the vast majority of the French people — 80 percent were peasants in 1814 — continued to live out lives shaped by folk custom and the almost unchanging forces of soil and climate, and the urban poor continued to lead lives determined largely by an unceasing and scarcely changing struggle for existence. For all they meant to these people in the *longue durée* of history Napoleon, the Consulate, the Empire might never have existed.

But many will still disagree. As the great Dutch historian, Pieter Geyl wrote, after studying the many and often conflicting French judgments of Napoleon, "History is an argument without end."

SUGGESTIONS FOR ADDITIONAL READING

The bibliography of Napoleon and the Consulate and Empire is enormous, and this essay can do no more than direct the reader's attention to some of the more important titles, largely those in English. The best introduction to Napoleonic historiography is Pieter Geyl, *Napoleon, For and Against* (New Haven, 1949), which surveys the writings in French on Napoleon from Mme. de Staël to Georges Lefebvre. Both more extensive and more exhaustive is Jacques Godechot, *L'Europe et l'Amérique à l'époque napoléonienne (1800-1815)*, Nouvelle Clio, No. 37, (Paris, 1967), which reviews the present state of scholarship on Napoleon and his times and cites more than five hundred titles. A brief introduction to the literature may be found in George F. Howe, *et al.*, eds., *The American Historical Association's Guide to Historical Literature* (New York, 1961). For a fuller bibliography, broken down into several categories, one may turn to the "Bibliographical Essay" in Geoffrey Bruun, *Europe and the French Imperium, 1799-1814* (New York, 1963), pages 251-272. To keep current of the steady flow of books and articles on Napoleon and the Empire one must use Jacques Godechot's bibliographical articles, which appear from time to time in the *Revue historique*.

Perhaps the best one-volume biography of Napoleon is August Fournier, *Napoleon the First, A Biography* (New York, 1925). There is a one-volume abridgment and translation into English of F. M. Kircheisen's monumental *Napoleon I, sein Leben und seine Zeit* (9 vols., Munich, 1911-1934); the English version is entitled *Napoleon* (New York, 1932). Other good biographies in English are J. Holland Rose, *The Life of Napoleon* (London, 1902), Jacques Bainville, *Napoleon* (Boston, 1933), J. M. Thompson, *Napoleon Bonaparte, His Rise and Fall* (New York, 1962), H. A. L. Fisher, *Napoleon* (2d ed.; New York, 1967), and Felix Markham, *Napoleon* (New York, 1963). Eugene Tarlé, *Bonaparte* (New York, 1937) is by a Russian Marxist. The best biography of Napoleon's first and more interesting Empress is Ernest J. Knapton, *Empress Josephine* (Cambridge, 1969).

Most of these volumes are more than simple biographies, dealing with both lives and times. Another group of books deals primarily with the times. Outstanding among them are Georges Lefebvre, *Napoleon from 18 Brumaire to Tilsit, 1799-1807* (New York, 1969) and *Napoleon from Tilsit to Waterloo, 1807-1815* (New York, 1969) and Geoffrey Bruun, *Europe and the French Imperium, 1799-1814*, cited above for its bibliography. Volume IX of *The New Cambridge Modern History, War and Peace in an Age of Upheaval, 1793-1814* (Cambridge, Eng., 1965), includes the years of the Consulate and Empire. For an important reappraisal and a synthesis of recent scholarship see *L'Episode napoléonienne (1799-1815): Aspects intérieurs* (Paris, 1972) by Louis Bergeron and *L'Episode napoléonienne (1799-1815): Aspects extérieurs* (Paris, 1972) by Jacques Lovie and A. Palluel-Guillard.

Two historians have attempted to reconstruct the story of Napoleon's life in his own words, drawing chiefly on his correspondence, which was published during the Second Empire: R. M. Johnston, *The Corsican* (Boston, 1930) and F. M. Kircheisen, *Napoleon's Autobiography* (New York, 1931). J. Christopher Herold has drawn on both Napoleon's written and his spoken words for his *The Mind of Napoleon* (New York, 1955), and J. M. Thompson has published translations of three hundred of Napoleon's letters in his *Napoleon's Letters* (Oxford, 1934). Recently an American publisher, AMS Press, reprinted all thirty-two volumes of the edition of 1858 of Napoleon's letters, *Correspondance de Napoléon* (New York, 1970).

On Napoleon's rise to power two titles are important: Spenser Wilkinson, *The Rise of General Bonaparte* (Oxford, 1930) and J. B. Morton, *Brumaire, the Rise of Bonaparte* (London, 1948).

The meteoric military career of Napoleon has attracted the attention of many authors. The most important recent volume is David Chandler, *The Campaigns of Napoleon* (New York, 1966). Henry Lachouque, *The Anatomy of Glory* (Providence, R.I., 1961) has a special appeal in its many color plates of uniforms of the Imperial Guard. Older titles that are still useful are Maximilien Yorck von Wartenburg, *Napoleon as a General* (2 vols., London, 1902) and T. A. Dodge, *Napoleon, a History of the Art of War from the Beginnings of the French Revolution to the Battle of Waterloo* (4 vols., Boston, 1904-1907). On the early years of Napoleon's military career see R. W. Phipps, *The Armies of the First French Republic and the Rise of the Marshals of Napoleon* (5 vols., Oxford, 1926-1939). Descriptions and analyses of individual campaigns or battles may be found in Harold T. Parker, *Three Napoleonic Battles* (Durham, 1944); Guglielmo Ferrero, *The Gamble, Bonaparte in Italy, 1796-97* (London, 1939); J. Christopher Herold, *Bonaparte in Egypt* (New York, 1963); A. B. Rodger, *The War of the Second Coalition, a Strategic Commentary* (Oxford, 1964); David Howarth, *Trafalgar: The Nelson Touch* (New York, 1969); Eugene Tarlé, *Napoleon's Invasion of Russia* (Oxford, 1942); Antony Brett-James, *1812: Eyewitness Accounts of Napoleon's Defeat in Russia* (New York, 1966); John Naylor, *Waterloo* (London, 1960); Christopher Hibbert, *Waterloo, Napoleon's Last Campaign* (New York, 1967). Leo Tolstoy's description of the Battle of Borodino in his *War and Peace* (New York, 1942) adds a new dimension to the military history of the Empire.

An introduction to Napoleon's role in the diplomacy of his time is provided by Robert Mowat, *The Diplomacy of Napoleon* (New York, 1924) and Felix Markham, *Napoleon and the Awakening of Europe* (London, 1954). Harold Deutsch, *The Genesis of Napoleonic Imperialism* (Cambridge, 1938) deals with the years 1800-1805, and a sequel is found in Herbert Butterfield, *The Peace Tactics of Napoleon, 1805-1808* (Cambridge, England, 1929). Eli Hecksher, *The Continental System, an Economic Interpretation* (Oxford, 1922), long the standard work on the subject, must now be used with Francois Crouzet, *L'Economie britannique et le blocus continental, 1806-1813* (2 vols., Paris, 1958). Valuable monographs dealing with particular aspects of consular and imperial diplomacy are Edward E. Y. Hales, *Napoleon and Pius VII* (London, 1962), and H. A. L. Fisher, *Studies in Napoleonic Statesmanship: Germany* (Oxford, 1903). Owen Connelly, *Napoleon's Satellite King-*

doms (New York, [c. 1965]) deals with the French rule of conquered neighbors.

Beyond the standard biographies and histories of the Consulate and the Empire little is available in English on Napoleon's domestic policies. Exceptions to the rule are Robert Holtman, *Napoleonic Propaganda* (Baton Rouge, 1950) and Henry Walsh, *The Concordat of 1801: A Study of the Problem of Nationalism in the Relations of Church and State* (New York, 1933). For *petite histoire* one may read Jean Robiquet *Daily Life in France under Napoleon* (London, 1963).

The final stages of Napoleon's career, from his arrival in Elba to his death on Saint-Helena, have attracted writers in every generation including the present. A. P. Herbert's *Why Waterloo?* (Garden City, 1953) is on Napoleon's months on Elba and why he was, in Herbert's opinion, forced to leave the island. On the Emperor's activities after his return to France, see Edith Saunders, *The Hundred Days* (London, 1963) and Antony Brett-James, ed., *The Hundred Days: Napoleon's Last Campaign from Eyewitness Accounts* (New York, 1965). The interval between the defeat at Waterloo and the arrival at Saint-Helena is the subject of Henry Lachouque's *The Lsst Days of Napoleon's Empire* (New York, 1967). Lord Rosebery considers the stormy years in exile on Saint-Helena in *Napoleon, the Last Phase* (London, 1900), which now must be used with Ralph Korngold, *The Last Years of Napoleon* (London, 1960). The question of the cause of Napoleon's death was reopened by Sten Forshufund, *Who Killed Napoleon?* (London, 1962). The best study in English of the Napoleonic Legend, a fruit of the years in exile, is Albert Guérard, *Reflections on the Napoleonic Legend* (New York, 1923), but Jean Tulard, *Le Mythe de Napoléon* (Paris, 1971), is superior.

The memoirs of men who worked closely with Napoleon can be very revealing of the character and personality of the man. Of special interest among those translated into English are the memoirs of the Duchess d'Abrantes and the Countess de Rémusat; General de Caulaincourt, *With Napoleon in Russia* (New York, [c. 1935]); Philippe de Ségur, *Napoleon's Russian Campaign* (Boston, 1958); and on the years on Saint-Helena the memoirs of Gourgaud, Las Cases, Montholon, and Bertrand.